NEW
ENGLAND
Village Life

NEW
ENGLAND
Village Life

By *EDWARD M. CHAPMAN*

BENJAMIN BLOM, INC.
Publishers New York 1971

First published Cambridge, Mass., 1937
Reissued 1971 by
Benjamin Blom, Inc.
New York, N.Y. 10025

Library of Congress
Catalog Card Number 73-174367 JUN 22 '72

Printed in the
United States of America

TO

THE ANCIENT CONNECTICUT TOWNS

OF

OLD SAYBROOK

AND

OLD LYME

IN

GRATEFUL

REMEMBRANCE

Preface

Caveat Lector! This is not a Treatise upon Rural Sociology. No 'Social Worker' has dipped his hand in it. No 'Investigator' from town has forced its story into his prepared pigeon-holes. The author has no wish to disparage these good people. He is simply confessing that this little book does not aspire to their realm of system and category. It makes little attempt to define or catalogue; and above all it is not the work of a stranger.

For a little over three hundred years the home of his family has maintained itself in one Connecticut community. For more than seventy-five years a daily record has been kept by the hand of one generation or another. It seemed worth while to sketch some phases of this life as it was actually lived by people of our neighbourhood and often of our intimate acquaintance — their work, play, sorrows, joys, modest successes and not infrequent failures.

Such simple annals could not, of course, be expected to interest the mass of readers brought up on more highly seasoned fare. It was inevitable too that some details of the story must be personal and intimate. Both of these considerations have inclined the writer toward private printing rather than publication. He has painted a picture of country life very different from that to which the readers of Mr. Dreiser or Miss Ferber are accustomed. But it is true. Moreover it is passing; and it deserves remembrance.

E. M. C.

WESTWAYS
NEW LONDON, CONNECTICUT
22 *May*, 1937

Contents

I

A Group of Village Men

THREE SAILORS

IT was in the early winter of 1831 that the new ship 'Samson,' Captain Daniel Chadwick, of Lyme, Connecticut, set sail from New York for London. Twenty-four days later she was safe in Portsmouth, England. A pretty good passage, it would seem to have been, so far forth. It did not seem so to her captain. Before me there lies a copy of his letter to his wife telling the story of the voyage.

'Dearest Nancy,' it begins; 'It has pleased kind Providence to protect the "Samson" and all in crew through a series of the most horrid accidents which could have occurred to any ship while at sea, and a safe passage to Portsmouth in 24 days.' Then follows the fragmentary story of what happened. The Captain had started to join his ship on a steamer, the 'Rufus King.' She 'burst her steam engine,' to use his own phrase, and he was obliged to transfer to the 'Napoleon.' Reaching the 'Samson,' all sail was made for sea. It was a tempestuous month in a tempestuous season, but the gales seem generally to have been westerly, and so far in his favour. But on December 5, when he could safely run no longer and was hove to, a sea carried away a boat and seems to have smashed both waist and quarter bulwarks.

Again on December 9, while scudding in Lat. 40° 50′ and Long. 40° 10′ — the reader will observe how completely this was in mid-Atlantic — a great following sea struck the ship, lifted the rudder with all its braces from the stern post, wrung it off from the rudder head under the counter, and in twenty minutes cleared it of the ship.

Think what this means. Here was a ship, new and untried, with a partial cargo of merchandise and a considerable fare of passengers. Here was a great gale raging at the stormiest season of the year when nights are longest. And here was the ship rudderless and helpless except as she could be guided by balancing her sails or by the poor expedient of a drogue.

Captain Chadwick at once set about building a new rudder of spars; built it with a heavy heart, I suspect, for there was little hope that he could hang it. Still, he built it; hailed a passing British ship, which furnished him some bolts; kept the 'Samson' going as best he might in her rudderless condition and in weather that continued to be heavy if not violent for four days after the accident. At last on December 13, the first day on which they had anything like moderate weather, to their own surprise and our wonder they succeeded in shipping this new rudder — actually slipped its pintles into their gudgeons, braced it, bent the tiller-ropes once more, and manned the wheel again.

Captain Chadwick is modest about it all. 'Had I been told previous to sailing,' says he, 'I could have made a rudder and shipped it at sea in a gale of wind I could not have believed it.' He casually refers to it to be sure as 'a great act'; and anyone who knows what it means to ship the rudder of an ordinary small boat in a seaway — a rudder perfectly fitted and weighing very likely but a dozen pounds — can dimly imagine the achievement of hanging a full-rigged ship's rudder, jury-built of spare spars, weighing many hundred pounds, and all under the counter of the ship in mid-Atlantic and in December storms.

This rudder worked better than its builders had dared to hope, though they trembled for its safety in every gale, and it guided them until December 20 found them in Lat. 49° 19′ and Long. 19° 20′, something like 850 miles from the English coast. There a tremendous squall fell upon the 'Samson,' with thunder, lightning, and hail. Sixteen men were on the foreyard, reefing, when lightning struck the foremast. It came down the foretopmast, carried away the chain slings of the foreyard, fortunately without injuring the men, followed the stanchions into the lower hold, and filled the ship with smoke and fear. They naturally thought themselves on fire, and searched anxiously for ten minutes, when, finding less smoke with no flame visible, they hoped the worst was over.

On clearing the forehatches to make sure, however, their fears were realized. In the lower hold the lightning had found cotton and turpentine in close conjunction, as though the malignant spirits of that wild night had scented out this most inflammable of combinations. With all possible haste they began to hoist out cargo, found the fire, and fortunately soon extinguished it. It had burned some cotton and eaten into the head of a barrel of turpentine stored beneath it, but had not eaten quite through. Only the mercy of Heaven and that remaining half-inch of oak, as Captain Chadwick thought, kept the ship from irretrievable disaster.

'The scene, dear Nancy,' says the letter, 'was more dreadful than I can describe, blowing a heavy gale and our ship on fire at three o'clock in the morning watch, though all our watches to me have been the same as I have scarcely left the deck during our passage.' The Captain ends upon an affectionate note very prettily phrased. 'Give my dear little children many kisses from me and you shall be repaid by your affectionate husband, D. Chadwick.' Then, true sailor and true Yankee that he was, there follows a postscript beginning, 'I can truly say I believe that had no accident occurred to us our passage would have been made in fourteen days.'

I should like to put beside this adventure of the early 'Thirties a voyage from England to America a generation later. The ship was a well-known and powerful one. Her captain's home was within a dozen miles of Captain Chadwick's. The documents are not at my hand but, as I have heard the story, word reached New York by cable or steamer that the 'Amazon'[1] had left Liverpool at her appointed time. It was winter, and a passage of less than thirty days could scarcely be expected. So the friends of officers and crew — and they were many in those days when boys were often entrusted to some well-known captain for training — settled down to wait without anxiety. When thirty days passed and no word came, still they were not anxious; nor did thirty-five or forty seem unduly long that winter. But when forty-five increased to fifty and fifty-five to sixty, anxiety grew keen with the slow-dragging hours. The time from sixty days to seventy saw hope become so dim that, as I have heard, only one man of sea-

[1] The following incident is based upon my memory of the report which was current in Essex — Captain Hovey's home — as repeated in my hearing by Mr. George W. Denison, who was teaching school in Essex at or about this time. Mr. Denison's interest in the sea was so deep and intelligent that I feel sure of the substantial accuracy of the report except for the identity of the ship.

authority in the home village dared cherish it. Yet at seventy days no assurance came either of safety or loss; nor at seventy-five.

It was not until the eightieth day had come and gone that word was flashed from Fire Island that the 'Amazon' had been sighted. She passed up through the Narrows, a sight to see and to remember — no battered and half-wrecked hulk, but still sound in hull and spars; and men wondered as they heard how Captain Hovey had threshed her across the whole width of the Western Ocean against a succession of heavy gales, and in cold so bitter as to force him to cut up the cabin carpets to make mittens for his crew. Yet her hull was tight, her spars unsprung, and every man was safe.

I am told that we do this same thing still and with far greater certainty of victory; and answer, 'Yes, by the sheer driving force of steam and steel.' But it is to be noticed that what this man did was to make a long and perilous voyage not merely in spite of the tempestuous elements that hindered him but by means of them. His enemies that sought to drive him back were the only agencies he had for getting on. They lay in wait to entrap him or marshalled all their hosts to overwhelm him. He made sail when he might and took in sail when he must. He caught them at their evil designs and turned them to his purpose. Sometimes their anger was so furious that he could only lie to and wait its passage. But generally he was edging on, under reefed topsails if he could do no more, sometimes on a better day shaking out his to'gallant sails only to clew them up a little later; always alert and vigilant, always tugging at those weary braces to make a sail lie flatter; always watchful of the wheel and the luff of his topsails if perchance he might bring his ship a half-point nearer to her course.

I submit that these things were real achievements. They illustrate that dominance of a man over things which almost always begins with the dominance of a man over himself. And they were of a type that distinctly influenced the life of many a New England village in the days of sail.

These men went far afield. I now turn to one who stayed at home — so close at home that to himself he must sometimes have seemed almost a prisoner there. Yet he too was a sailor.

In Long Island Sound five miles off the old town of Guilford lies Faulkner's Island. Its surface is a matter of only a few acres, but it rises high above the sea and its lighthouse is of importance. It is important as a warning against the reefs and rocks by which the island is surrounded, and even more as a way-mark to vessels laying their courses to and from New York — for Long Island Sound is a great thoroughfare. On that little island separated from the main land by so broad a strip of tideway, Oliver Brooks lived for thirty-one years. There he set up his home. There with such necessary absences as were required, first for being born and afterward for being sent to school, his children were reared.

It must have sometimes seemed a narrow and cabined life to those who lived it. I never thought it so, looking in as I was privileged to do upon their pleasant home and the gracious dignity and courtesy of Captain and Mrs. Brooks. Their island was small enough, to be sure; there is a big bluff on the east rising abruptly from the Sound, and a little slope of greensward on the west stretching down to a tiny boat landing. That is all. But every night for thirty-one years those people kept their light shining over the busy waters guiding ships and safeguarding human lives. If by day their range seemed limited, by night they held converse with a wide and often a very needy world.

Of course there were visits to the mainland; and in summer visitors came to the island. Pleasant and memorable interludes took place. It was from the foot of that lighthouse on an early summer morning in 1881 that when little more than a boy I saw the famous frigate 'Constitution' dropping down Sound under sail — the last voyage, I suspect, that she ever made under her own power — and I still seem to see how lofty her royals and how deep her to'gallant sails were.

But there were other interludes which verged on tragedy. During those thirty-one years, about one hundred wrecks took place in the neighbourhood of the island; and in seventy-one of these cases Captain Brooks helped save life. Sometimes the task was simple enough and any competent boatman might have done it. Sometimes it was desperate, and only a clear head, a very stout heart, and first-rate seamanship could avail. These he could bring to meet it, and all were demanded when on November 23, 1858, the 'Moses Webb' went ashore on Goose Island, a clump of rocks about a mile to westward of the light. The crew took to the rigging and clung there helpless. It was a dreadful chance for one man in an open boat to take in the gale that was blowing, and when Oliver Brooks started, they say that he too, like Captain Chadwick, was moved to kiss his wife and children as though his journey were likely to be a long one. I am pretty sure he did not expect to get back that day, even if he lived to get back at all, for he is said to have gathered a few simple supplies as though to tide him and the shipwrecked whom he might rescue over a night spent on Goose Island.

But
> 'Sudden the worst turns the best to the brave.'

He ran to leeward without mishap; found enough of a lee, I suppose, under the wreck to allow him to work, and one by one, as the sea permitted, succeeded in rescuing five persons, four men and a woman, from the 'Webb's' rigging.[1] More than that he actually got them back to his home and his wife's care before the day was done.

I like to look back upon those people as I knew them; the Captain active, almost nervously alert to all that went on in the sky above and the waters beneath, yet not exactly a hurried man; composed and quiet rather, though rarely relaxed. He was a man, too, of a genuine comeliness; somewhat slight in build but of an admirably twisted fibre, and with a face that bespoke keen intelligence, a habit of mastery over circumstance, true reverence for all good things, and an abounding humour. I always hesitate to illustrate a man's humour because the quality itself so certainly evaporates in the process. I shall not attempt to show forth Captain Brooks on this side of his nature because it cannot be adequately done. But when I say that he could take quaint and whimsical liberties with Nature herself and carry the business through to a happy conclusion, I at least suggest something of his resourcefulness and force of character.

Here an illustration or two may help. The Captain was a pretty good musician in a modest way, while his daughters were rather accomplished mistresses, the one of the piano and the other of the violin or 'cello. In their trios he carried the double bass, and still sometimes there comes back to me a September afternoon when they played

[1] There was, I think, one casualty in the death of a child, which very likely occurred before the arrival of the rescuer.

together in their pleasant parlour. I see them all intent upon their instruments, and somehow fitting into the peace which brooded upon the sea and their little island rising from it.

But to come back to my illustrations. When not accompanying his daughters, the Captain played the flute; nor did he altogether disdain the fife. He had at this time a large and intelligent dog of great dignity of bearing. This dog he had taught to 'sing,' as by courtesy it was called. A chair was placed in which the dog seated himself, crossing his big paws over the arm. The flute began its mild accompaniment; and then at the proper time (or a little before or after it), the dog started a series of the most astonishing noises that I ever heard. They were not the long-drawn howls of canine distress; nor yet were they ordinary barks, but a wonderful something in between. The vocalisation, moreover, was very marked. The dog not only opened a capacious mouth, but opened it capaciously and shut it with decision quite in the accepted manner, and was undoubtedly a little influenced in the tempo of his preposterous performance by his master's flute.

If the thing seem rather dreadful in the telling, that is my fault. One should have seen it: the whimsical earnestness of the Captain blowing and fingering his flute, anxious that his dog should do its best; the fluttering half-remonstrance of his well-bred daughters; all dominated by the dignity of the splendid dog rendering his absurd and intolerable song. Never, outside of Congress, do I remember to have heard such nonsense uttered with the mien of Jove.

Captain Brooks was also a man of considerable scientific knowledge; something of an authority upon birds and fishes; well known to men of high standing in learned circles; occasionally consulted by the Smithsonian Institution, I believe, with reference to his observations; and with it all a very deft taxidermist. His collection of birds was notable. In making it he had shot a great snowy owl, a rare subarctic visitor, but unfortunately had so seriously injured the bird's head as to unfit it for mounting. It looked for the moment as though much wild life and beauty must be wasted. But the Captain had an inspiration. Just at that time he had killed from among his fowls a very fine cock, and he at once set about joining this rooster's golden head to the owl's snowy shoulders. No other man would have thought of such a thing; few men could have done it. But at the bidding of his whimsical mind and under his skilful fingers there arose one of the most arresting and yet beguiling monsters that ever was seen. I have watched a competent naturalist gaze at it in amazement for an appreciable time before it revealed itself and the inevitable laugh came.

This playing tricks with Nature is not a pleasant thing to contemplate in the abstract. Yet here was a man so simple, so brave, so humorous, so whimsical, and with it all so skilful that he was able, in the slang of the day, 'to carry it off.' He was an uncommonly resourceful man who had proved his mettle time and again when human lives hung in the balance; but his playfulness was like the playfulness of a child. He was a man who would have acquitted himself with credit if not with distinction in almost any position for which he might have been trained — one of those men whom it required no effort to think of as sitting on the judge's bench, or speaking from the preacher's pulpit, or standing as an ambassador before kings. Special training would have been needed, I repeat; but here were adequate mental and moral materials to be trained. His wife matched him admirably with her domestic and motherly tastes and her calming influence upon his energetic and sometimes nervous habit.

Such were the man and woman who spent their working lives cooped up on that three or four acres of upland in Long Island Sound. It may sometimes have seemed to them as though they were fitted for larger things and ought to have had a wider scope. Others must have thought so. I doubt it. The strength of our older New England lay in the fact that it could command such people for such tasks. It might be the better for us if such tasks still appealed to such people.

A Group of Village Men

THREE LANDSMEN

THE three sailors of the last chapter were set in the foreground of my picture of village life for several reasons. They helped to give the village a wider outlook than it would otherwise have had. Of this something will be said later on. Then too, despite their long and frequent absences, they and their families had distinct part and lot in village life. One of Captain Chadwick's daughters married the village clergyman. His son became the village lawyer, but with a reputation and a practice that far surpassed both town and county bounds. One grandson was an active member of the commission that brought the Catskill Mountain water into New York, and despite the vicissitudes of New York politics saw that great task through; while another became a well known Federal judge.

Captain Hovey was respected for the sake of his father, the village minister, as well as for his own. His comings and goings were matters of public moment, and the whole community grieved when during the perilous transition from sail to steam he was involved in one of its numerous disasters and lost his life off the coast of Florida.

Captain Brooks came to the mainland, lived to a good old age, fitted as he was bound to do into the village life, and represented his fellow citizens for one or more terms in the Legislature.

Now we pass on to a very different type of life. It was like that which has just been sketched in seeming cabined and confined. It was unlike it in being devoid of outward adventure. I do not know whether I shall be easily forgiven for including a country merchant in my list of worthies. Yet here he is. There isn't exactly any name for him. One cannot describe him as a grocer, because he sold fabrics; nor can one call him a draper, because his basement was filled with salt, sugar, and molasses and his little upper attic with shoes. The only way to epitomize such a man is to say simply 'that he kept a store'; and as one says it the thing itself appears to the mind's eye in all its fascinating dinginess — this *omnium gatherum* of coffee, sugar, tea, molasses, pepper, ginger, candy, hardware, grain, flour, collars, calico, boots and shoes.

I never count the time lost when forced to wait in a general store. I look and wonder at the multitude of things men use and at the genius which has assembled them in one place; and the wonder grows at the gifts of mind that can keep their places and prices in memory, and the gifts of body that can hasten from the loading of a barrel of flour to the selling of a paper of pins, and endure the varied process all day long. By general consent keeping a country store represents the acme of humdrum existence (if a humdrum existence can, indeed, have any acme). I confess that it seems so to me, though I should incline to prefer it to a shop in town.

Yet admitting all this, I confidently introduce my general storekeeper. He was a very quiet man, as such men often are. He kept his own books, as such men generally must. He kept them more neatly than many books are kept, and in a notably firm and exact hand that suggested the man-stuff under the unobtrusive surface and quiet address. He had been born in a somewhat remote district of the town in which he did his life work. He had married the daughter of a not very distant neighbour, as was the frequent New England custom. He began business in a very small way, I think with a relative. Soon set up for himself, again in a small way. Continued with quiet success until he was an old man in what many other men would have thought a small way still. He never accumulated large wealth but gained a modest competence.

He never of course attained large place or attracted wide attention; and equally of course he could not travel much. I suppose there were whole years in which he scarce went farther from his store than to the county town fifteen miles away in which he did his banking. He had a pleasant home opposite his place of business upon the main village street, which he kept with conspicuous neatness; and almost the only recreation I ever saw him take beyond an occasional drive with some member of his family was in working about his grounds or the street in front of them.

By the house and store there sometimes passed very able and some brilliant men. Out of the house next door came a Chief Justice of the United States. To the house beyond that a famous man who afterward became President of the United States brought his family for an occasional summer. Next door to that lived for several years a clergyman who came later to be known in two continents as a foremost New Testament critic. Next again stood the house of a Chief Justice of the State who had at one time, as *chargé d'affaires*, represented the United States at the Court of Vienna. Then, crossing the street and going but one house further, you found the residence of a professor of Sanskrit in a great university, and the teacher of two of the most famous scholars that America has produced. That was a notable village street and these men, every one of them, must have entered our friend's doors; while perhaps after one of them there might have come a group of artists — for that little town of scarce twelve hundred souls was a famous rendezvous for artists and their pupils. The best of all these men knew James Rowland for what he was; but some casual summer visitor, knowing him but a little, might have thought his life narrow and his soul meagre.

Now, I am not trying to make heroes out of my sheaf of plain men. In a sense the life was narrow; though in no sense was the soul meagre. For see what this man did. He bought and sold the products of many trades and climes. He bought and sold with so strict a sense of accountability to God above and neighbour man beside him that his honour became almost a proverb. Shrewd he was, I think, in his buying and selling, but never predominantly shrewd. The adjective came late in your description of him. Men trusted him and he deserved their trust. He was considerate of the poor. He liked the serviceable character of his calling. A conscience went into what he bought and sold. He ruled some things out of his list of goods though they were in excellent demand, because he thought their tendency was dissipating rather than constructive. He was, too, a religious man who felt that his place and work here were assigned him by a Master with reference to some large plan to the end of which he himself could not see. So though modest-minded he never despised himself or his business or any man who served him. No useful thing could seem quite despicable to him indeed.

On the contrary, he exerted an influence wider than he ever knew that made for self-respect and competence among younger men whose lives he had touched.

Sunday was one of the institutions that kept his life from becoming petty. Then, however busy and fretting the week had been, this man was redeemed from littleness by his meditations upon high themes. He was an officer in the old Established Church of Connecticut — the Congregational; reverent in his worship and constant in his service. Sometimes in meetings for that purpose he would lift up his quiet voice to lead his fellows in prayer. A quiet voice it still remained, but in its accents echoing against the background of so gracious and faithful a life one heard a man speaking with Him who 'leadeth forth the seven Stars and Orion and turneth the shadow of death into the morning.' And when I hear men speak disparagingly of shopkeepers as though their only pursuit were dollars and all their activities were selfish I like to think of this man, his high ideals, his genuine service and his constructive influence in the community. The selling of butter, cheese, and papers of pins is not an exalted office; but it is a very necessary office, and when filled honestly and serviceably the man who fills it looms a good deal larger than many a critic, be he never so clever.

Very briefly and inadequately I must now notice the fifth man in my group of six. He too is an exemplar of what is generally thought to be the quiet life. A country minister, he spent practically the whole of a long working day in one town. He was well born to begin with, and that is much; and he was excellently educated, which is often more. His family belonged to old stock. It had roots, traditions, permanence; and it had courage with the spirit of industrial adventure. That family became known almost the world around for its efficiency in devising, improving, and always honestly making, the Fairbanks scale.

Into one branch of such a serviceable race this man was born. His immediate family had means rather than money. The distinction is real. They had a competence. They had enough to do with. And that was what they valued a competence for — to *do* with, not to make a show of or to rest at ease upon. It was not a large competence, but it sufficed. So this boy was sent to excellent schools and later to Yale University. After an honourable career in these places there was an interlude of foreign travel and study which took him to Egypt, Arabia, and Syria, then less visited than now, opened his kind and humorous eyes to many ways and many men, and brought him home to the work of the Christian ministry. For this too he had first-rate training in the schools of divinity; and beyond that there was in him a very vital faith in the best things, a deep desire to be of use to men, a thorough liking and sympathy for them, and a quite unique gift of imagination which gave to both his written and spoken words a pungency sweet, memorable, and wholesome as the savour of the spruce and pine he loved.

He settled in a little parish in his native town; served a notable apprenticeship there; was called and went after a few years to a larger church — the church with which his immediate family was connected — in the same township, though in a larger village of it; and there spent the remainder of his professional life. Yet I do not like that word 'professional' very well. We are too apt to apply it to men whose humanity is lost in their conventions — whose essence is somehow held subject to their environment. This man always seemed to dominate his circumstances.

He was a parson — almost unmistakeably that; a country parson, moreover, who never appeared to desire to be anything else. He was conservative in many of his tastes and in some of his views of life and faith; but he was radical too in loving the roots of things, the essences of life, the souls of people, all the deep and lastingly significant aspects of our being here and our belonging to one another; things which too few professed radicals seem to care much about. So he lived for many decades until the time came when he felt that he must give up his church. But he could not go away. Neither was he willing nor could the community spare him. So he stayed as the head of an institution known as the Athenaeum — a combined library, art museum, and purveyor of all good things to the neighbourhood.

A pleasant, worthy, rather humdrum life, you say. I answer, a life of high and often enchanting adventure. This man's body stayed generally at home except for his year or two of foreign study and travel. But the mind and soul of him were always extraordinarily alert and active. He knew the secrets of men's hearts. He was alert to note the manners and matters of the common day. Birds sang, flowers bloomed, clouds floated in the sky, rain watered the earth, snow mantled and blanketed it, Spring was born again, and Autumn bore its fruits just as though all were done for this man. I do not mean that he was a selfish or in any way a self-centered man. He was not; but all these beings and doings of the world spoke to him. Scarce a wind blew by him but whispered in his ear some message that fed his soul and helped him feed the souls of others.

For a man of his very high order of intelligence, I do not think he was particularly shrewd in dealing with people. He had too much business of a better sort on hand to stop to be shrewd. You might cheat him, if you had a chance, once or twice — you could not many times; but set him on horseback and let him ride among the hills and fields; let him walk up the village street where all knew and loved him, and you found him so wise and clear-eyed that shrewdness seemed but a sham wisdom after all. For he could read the face of the world, and he could see into the hearts and high destinies of men.

He was, for instance, once meditating and writing about life's mysteries when suddenly a fly alighted on his paper. Another would have brushed the annoying thing away, but this man was just whimsical enough to put him into his address. Here he is:

'A fly just alighted rubs his antennae sleekly, drops his fore paws, desires to know what I am writing about. Good fly, I was just this moment saying how impossible it would be for God to explain to me the high mysteries of His thoughts.'

Here too is a pregnant question based on some incident of travel. 'Why can you not pocket the advantage when the conductor forgets your ticket? Because of a heavenly vision that paints honor in more radiant colors than profit, and holds the least item in each day's duty sacred as it were the jewel of an angel's crown.' Or again, 'Mahogany takes finer polish than pine, but that doesn't discredit pine. Seest thou one that is bass-woody? Know then that if the Lord made him so, he is made for a purpose and ought to fit somewhere excellently well.' Even his morning looking-glass reflected the world. 'There is no sense,' he says, 'in poking at the mirror as though it were merely the device of feminine vanity. Everyone must come to it to know if he is presentable. It serves to put a finer face on humanity. It deserves respect for telling the truth. Yea, what is this Bible mirror for if not to dress by?'

So all his life his soul was having its adventures sometimes amid green pastures and by still waters, and sometimes in 'perilous seas, in faëry lands forlorn.'   He
delighted in the adventure for its own sake, and for the
confirmation of his faith which it always seemed to furnish.
Men, women, and children loved him and were the better
for him. The fact that his long and useful life was thus
ploughed into the soil of his native town assured a better
harvest of life's best things for each later generation. He
helped greatly to enhance the sum of what Edward
Fitzgerald once called 'the funded virtues of many good
men gone by.'

Thus we come to the last of our six men. He and his calling represent very fundamental things, and the reader can
guess that he is a farmer. But how, it may be asked, can
a farm and the farmer be made interesting? The so-called
humorous papers seem to know; so do the cheap burlesques
and the almost equally cheap though better-meant sentimental comedies. One recalls the type of 'hayseed' therein
depicted — the grotesque dress, the outlandish speech, the
unfailing corncob pipe, the general slackness of surroundings and limitation of outlook, the shrewdness that so often
aims at overreaching or the good nature that is loveable,
to be sure, but at the same time a little laughable. Now
the man whom I have in mind may not have been a typical
New England farmer. I know that he was a real New
England farmer. No man in all the world had a better
right to be called so; for he farmed land that had been in
his family's possession for more than two hundred years,
and he lived in one of the oldest New England towns, of
which his direct ancestor had been an original settler.
Under these circumstances the reader may think I am

describing one with whom farming was only an avocation — not something by which he won his living. No, I am not. To be sure, this man inherited and saved some capital; but it was small as compared with the heavy demands made upon his purse. He also had some other interests beside his farming; but these represented liabilities as often as assets. Primarily and almost exclusively he was a farmer, getting his support and that of his family out of the soil, which he tilled with his own hands, and which he tilled exceedingly well.

Yet this man was not in any one particular the analogue of the farmer in whom the paragrapher or caricaturist delights. When working in the field he dressed accordingly, and sometimes clung to old clothes beyond what wife and daughters thought to be wise or seemly; but never in his most careless moments did he affect overalls hung precariously by one suspender, or a broad-brimmed hat reaching to his shoulders. You could not force a broad-brimmed hat upon him; nor did he, except when the nature of his work compelled it, stick his trousers into his boot-tops; and as for the corncob or any other sort of pipe, I doubt if any other class of men — certainly among those whose work is considerably laborious — so generally abstained from tobacco in all its forms as the substantial farmers whom I have known in southern Connecticut.

Nor was it possible to imagine his mouth uttering the outlandish speech of the book-and-paper farmer. He spoke two languages, as so many high-class countrymen do; one was the vernacular used with his workmen or in discussion of farm affairs — a vernacular that was neither vulgar in the sense of being low nor ungrammatical, except as some colloquialisms cannot well be parsed. The other language was just as natural to him; but it was the speech of more serious occasions, when the form as well as the substance of discourse claimed the speaker's attention, or when a letter was to be written. Then I do not think that I have ever heard any man use better English; better, I mean, in its adaptation to its ends, so crystal-clear was it, so free from affectation or any needless ornament or any striving for effect. It may sometimes have been a little old-fashioned in pronunciation, but it was altogether free from the absurd vowel sounds that the books foist upon farmers. This man could no more have said 'caouw' or 'naow' than he could have used 'darn' or 'gosh' or 'by heck' or any other vulgar expletive.

In conversation when his interest was aroused the voice, like most of our American voices, tended to be high. In any public meeting on the rare occasions when he addressed one, it was restrained and beautifully modulated. This, like the admirable propriety and felicity of his speech on such occasions, seemed to be due less to any forethought than to an instinctive respect for his fellows and for himself.

The farmer of our pictures generally has a straggling, weedy beard. This man's beard was thick and rather short, like those one sees on Roman coins or statues; and I mention this because it was characteristic of something in the physical and mental habit of the man. He was lean and rather tall, admirably proportioned and well knit; his mind was singularly judicial and his speech *ad rem* — always *ad rem*. I doubt if he would have made a good lawyer, because he would have shrunk from the rivalries and contentions of the courtroom, and the necessity of presenting one side of a case to a jury would have involved positive pain. But could he have obtained the necessary training in some other way he must have made an admirable judge, so keen was his instinct for truth on the one hand and sham on the other, and so admirably balanced was his mind.

He showed here certain defects of his qualities and was a little lacking in initiative. If small things went against him he was too apt to revise his own position with some discouragement and a little self-pity, instead of revising the things. If workmen were slack or could not be had, he was a little down-daunted, and would perhaps consider changing his plans for work instead of correcting the slackness or going far enough afield to find his needed man. But despite these things, and the further limitation that he was no mechanic and did not try to be one, he was a capital farmer. Interestingly, he grew progressive as he grew old, and owing in no small degree to his wife, who had not only high intelligence and an excellent education, but power of initiative enough for her own realm and for his too, his farming adapted itself to changed conditions, took advantage of new machineries, methods, and markets, and in his old age exerted a considerable influence by example upon the community.

Though in no sense a trained naturalist, he was not only a keen but a highly intelligent observer of the world in which and on which he wrought. He knew the ways of birds and beasts, of winds and tides, since his was a coast farm, of trees and flowers, and the secrets of keeping crops and particularly of selecting seed. It was characteristic of his admirable balance that no one could sow with a more even hand. This was a task he scarce ever entrusted to a subordinate, and he would even go himself to sow for a neighbour, not only as an accommodation but because he knew that he could do it well and he loved to see the grain come up even and strong. I wonder sometimes at the genuine learning that such a man acquires in the course of a long life; a learning so instinct with wisdom that it will force us sometime to revise our estimates of education.

Two characteristics remain to be noted. He was deeply religious on the one hand, and on the other he had the largest capacity for humorous nonsense of any really serious man I ever knew. His somewhat grave demeanor in public misled the casual onlooker, and I still hear the ironical laughter of some member of his household upon being asked if he were not rather a stern man in his family. Instead of that, he was so playful with little children that at bedtime they sometimes had to be dragged out of his arms lest such ecstatic fun should murder sleep; and he had an unmeasured store of whimsical answers to their questions. Such things do not bear repetition. But I heard a child who had been to the sea once ask him if porpoises did any harm; to which his instant and sufficient answer was that he had never heard of their robbing orchards. This reply and the tone of its utterance not only answered the question by clearing the porpoise of suspicion, but left a pleasing glow in the child's mind as its fancy played with the idea of that sleek burgomaster of the sea laboriously and sinfully swarming up a tree after apples.

This man was a Puritan in the sense that he took conscience into account in all he did; but he was not a precisian in the sense of taking peddling and artificial care of trifles. There was room in his nature as there was room in his conversation for the necessary give and take of life; and therein he was, I believe, typical of the best of the Puritans, who seem to me to have been caricatured by history very much as the farmer is caricatured by the cartoonist. That some of the Puritan settlers had abounding humour, I know; that many of them possessed it, I believe; and we all know that it is most appetizing when cleansed of cynicism and representing the play of mind natural to a man of courage, reverence, and faith.

It was so with him. You could not account for him — his strength, his real learning, his justice, his humility, his playfulness, except upon the ground of his faith in God, in the essential worth of men and his quiet respect for himself. He too was an officer in the church, to which eight generations of his family had belonged, and he was devoted to its welfare and that of the message which it proclaimed — devoted to the point of sacrifice. Yet he inclined to reticence about the things that moved him most. Once I chanced to be in Washington with him on one of the few journeys that he made outside New England. We went the rounds of the city, the public buildings and Mount Vernon, sometimes finding groups of curious tourists, and sometimes by ourselves. His interest was keen but very quiet, and at last one day when we had seen apartments where history had been made, he said to me not without emotion: 'When I'm in places like these I don't feel like saying anything. I want to keep still and look and think.' [1]

That was quite characteristic of the deep pieties and reverences of this man. Something of it spoke in all these lives that I have tried to sketch. And they have been brought together, not because they were widely known or pre-eminently gifted, but because they are typical of large groups of men in every section of our country with whom

---

[1] A half-dozen sentences of the characterization of this Farmer are paraphrased from the opening chapter of one of the Author's earlier books; which has, however, been so long out of print that none of its infrequent readers is likely to accuse him of repetition.

are the hidings of our Nation's power. Some of them will appear again on later pages, and to the Farmer I shall be compelled to make repeated reference in the chapters dealing with farm-life, not for the sake of exalting a very modest man but because his diaries throw so clear a light upon my theme.

III

The Farmer-Fisherman

THE late Edward Douglass White, while Chief Justice of the United States, once told me that in his early years on the Bench of the Supreme Court he visited Rhode Island as the guest of Mr. Rowland Hazard of Peacedale. His host took him for a drive along the shore of Narragansett Bay. They passed various farms. None was large, and so few were fertile that Mr. White wondered how their occupants maintained themselves. At last he put the question to Mr. Hazard. The latter directed his attention to the shore and the fact that here and there along it boats were drawn up each as near as might be to some little homestead. With them, he said, lay the secret. These farms had, it was true, limited acreage, no very great fertility, and but indifferent cultivation. They offered their owners, however, a supply of food, summer pasture and winter hay for horse and cow, enough odds and ends for pig and fowls, fuel from a little woodlot, and — quite as significant as anything else — a home and the sense of owning it. The boat and what it stood for did the rest.

The thing lay quiescent in the mind of the eminent Judge; but some time later, when the question of confiscating certain small craft captured and claimed as prizes during our war with Spain reached the Supreme Court, it awoke memories and helped to furnish arguments that, he told me, materially influenced the decision of the case and the return of the boats to their owners.

What Mr. Justice White and his host saw in Rhode Island might have been duplicated on various sections of the Connecticut seaboard, but nowhere more significantly than in the region of the noble river from which the State takes its name. Here shad ruled the spring. There were, to be sure, farmers with acres and interests enough to occupy them exclusively. There were, too, fishermen whose living winter and summer alike was won almost as exclusively from the sea. But between these came a class of amphibians whose activities, whether on land or water, had for me an unfailing charm, and who are now gone from the coast almost to a man. All fish interested them to a greater or less degree; but it was *Alosa sapidissima* who put money in their somewhat meagre purses, educated their children, paid their mortgages, and gave yearly variety to their laborious and somewhat humdrum lives.

There was a time when this fish was so abundant as to be lightly esteemed; when the salmon, too, in Southern Connecticut was so plentiful as to become an object almost of loathing to those who ate it perforce; so that there may well be some historical foundation to the legend that, under the indentures of old-time apprentices, salmon might not be served to them more than so often a week. It is practically certain that about the mouth of the Connecticut the too frequent use of shad fresh or salted once seemed like a badge of improvidence and implied a scarcity of pork in the family larder. I should like to have asked my own Great-Grandfather, who on his return from the French and Indian and Revolutionary Wars was one of a committee to 'dignify' the pews in church — a most unchristian practice — whether, in determining the social standing of his fellow worshippers, he actually did take their dependence upon shad into account as tradition says was done.

Perhaps it was this that brought about a dispute with a disgruntled neighbour who interviewed the old gentleman one day while he was out about his farm. The grievance was duly aired and discussed until the 'dignifier' of pews finally said: 'Go home, Mr. X; go home. You have as good a seat in church as you deserve.' The remonstrant shot a Parthian arrow: 'Maybe so! But I'd have you know, Captain, that if we all had our deserts, some of us would get a seat no nearer the House of God than the town pound.' This was more than the irascible old officer could stand, and he advanced upon the malcontent; who, however, had prudently chosen his ground upon the farther side of a little creek, so that the incident ended in flight and safety.

The earliest mode of taking shad was doubtless by a short hauling seine operated by hand from seashore or river bank. As the industry increased and both the domestic and market value of the fish, fresh in the spring and salted for the winter, was enhanced, three methods came into use all of which were common in my boyhood.

The first of these was simply a high development of the primitive seine. Anyone who has navigated the lower reaches of the Connecticut knows how needful it is to keep a sharp lookout for the artificial 'piers' where the capstans that hauled these mighty nets once stood. Running up from the bar and carrying the two lights at the river's mouth in line, the sailor would find himself almost on top of 'Gibraltar.' It lies well out from shore on the edge of the Lyme flats, with its two heaps of stone awash or quite covered at high tide, and has been long since deserted. But it was busy enough at certain times of tide in the old days. The fish-house stood on a little wooded 'hammock' in the edge of the salt meadow to the eastward. There the boats were moored and there the simple appurtenances of the industry were kept. There too the fishermen lived during the season except for week-ends spent at home.

The process of fishing was as simple in plan as it was laborious. A large boat carried out a net of great length and considerable depth from one of the two piers. After it was shot a smaller boat — and excellent craft the best of these were — carried the hauling lines to a capstan on the other pier. Then by a long march round this capstan the big net was recovered, sometimes with few and some-times in the old days with exceeding many and very beautiful fish.

I have called this a simple and laborious process. To hear it thus briefly described or even to see it done might lead the onlooker to think that anyone of adequate muscle and industry could do it. This is a common mistake in regard to the processes of farm and shore. In point of fact, the successful management of one of these great nets near the mouth of the river, where springtime freshets were complicated by tide-currents, was a business demanding experience and judgement with knowledge of wind and tide in high degree. The man who got his net into the strength of a tide-stream might find it taking command of his capstan and trying to go to sea instead of coming in. Strange tales are told of capstan bars whirling at their own will with one man riding a perilous merry-go-round and another trying to dodge it. Or, if no mishap of this sort occurred, a swirling current might form a pocket in the net that would be difficult to clear, or that would shorten its effective length, or, worst of all, release the partially impounded fish. That the lead-line must be kept down and the cork-line not dragged under was evident to the feeblest intellect, but like so many other evident things not always easy of accomplishment.

The second method, and one still in vogue, though thought by some to be doomed to a lingering death, is that commonly called gill-net fishing or dragging. The name might suggest some form of hauling seine. Yet in fact the dragnet was and is a delicate affair of twine strong enough to hold an eight- or ten-pound fish, and still fine enough to be unnoticed at night or in the thick water of a spring freshet. It is fished by one boat and two men, who set it in some well-known reach of the River, drift with it so far as seems advisable, lift it for the capture of such fish as are caught by the gills, and set it once more for another drift.

A simple matter again, thinks the uninitiated. But let the uninitiated try it in the reach of a river whose shoals, rocks, and currents are unknown to him; at night, moreover, when other craft are about and when a steamer is due; perhaps in fog or storm, and, if it be a lower reach, very possibly in a considerable seaway, and he is likely to realize as he ruefully surveys a net torn by rock and driftwood or cut in twain by a steamer that things are not what they seem. He had thought to catch fish. He finds that to do so he must first save and rightly serve a net; and that this will often involve long hours of mending and reknitting as well as careful drying on a reel.

The third method, and to me the best known of all in boyhood, was that of the 'pound' or 'trap.' Of the three, this involved the largest measure of outlay and preparation. In the case of the larger pounds it also required a more extended service of boats — a large decked scow for driving 'stakes' at the beginning and pulling them at the end of the season, a big flat-bottom 'sharpie' for hauling the pound and carrying fish, and a smaller boat for tending lines and general utility purposes. There was a rough house on shore where sometimes the fishermen stayed; indeed if the place were at all remote one or two men would live there.

The land of my Grandfather and Father, extending from our homestead some three quarters of a mile to the sea, held such a house on its margin, and a modest rental was paid by one of the larger companies of fishermen for its use and the privilege of landing and packing fish in and about it. Though a smelly place during the fishing season, it had abundant charms to soothe boyhood's breast, and when fishing was over it was duly cleansed and used as a bathhouse in the summer.

The pound as I knew it has pretty nearly if not quite disappeared. Traps of a similar sort are still in abundant use; but they are less in size and somewhat different in form. The big pound of my boyhood was a majestic affair, which as a whole might reach a half-mile or more from the beginning of its leader to the outer rim of its last bowl. The sketch on page 33 will show the scheme of the pound in rough outline. Its fundamental principle was that while the shad is a fish of well-developed instinct, it is not a creature of much intellectual power. This instinct moved it, when swimming alongshore toward the mouth of the Connecticut and its spawning grounds in fresh water, to turn seaward on meeting any obstacle. Such an obstacle the 'leader' of the pound provided by

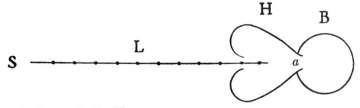

S. Shore or Shallow Water.

L. Leader, perhaps ¼ mile long in large pounds.

H. Heart — Note re-entrant angles at base to turn a fish off shore.

B. Bowl, with floor as well as sides of net. In hauling, an apron at *a* is raised closing the entrance; the fish are cooped in one segment of the Bowl by overhauling the floor, and then bailed into the boat by scoop-nets.

stretching a long line of net, or 'twine' as it was called, supported on heavy poles and reaching from shallow water into that of considerable depth. This 'twine' was a fixture and stood from one end of the season to the other, except as it was taken up from time to time for drying and replaced by spare sections. Its sole purpose was to turn the fish toward the business end of the pound. They swam alongshore and on finding their path blocked went obediently seaward.

In thus following the 'leader' they came next to the 'heart.' Like the leader, this was designed to catch nothing of itself, but only to guide the simple shad into further and fatal difficulty. It consisted of pound-poles driven in the shape of a rough heart; and upon these a permanent wall of netting was stretched. This heart was a partial enclosure with open entrances at the broad and deeply encised base and an open exit at the apex.

Into the middle of the base the leader led. There the fish swimming seaward entered the heart. After she was in there was nothing to prevent her from turning and going out as she had come — nothing, that is, but her exceeding simple mind and her instinct for deeper water. Instinct she worshipped like a Freudian, and so followed the leader into the heart. Well within the gate into the lobes the leader stopped, and the fish was free to move about the heart-shaped enclosure. There was nothing there to catch her. Let us suppose that becoming anxious she decided to turn back along the side of the heart. She could freely do so; but as she came to the opening at the base of the lobe and approached the gate through which she had entered, the deep incision of the lobes turned her seaward again, instinct reasserted itself, and off she swam toward deeper water and the exit at the apex into the bowl.

Here there was an open gate again, but over it, if *Alosa* could but read, there might well have been inscribed the old Dantean motto about leaving hope behind. When her silver beauty had glanced through those gateposts she was in an enclosure which had bottom as well as sides of 'twine,' and the gate behind could and would be closed. To be sure, it would stay open until slack water tomorrow morning, and theoretically it could be repassed; but her toothsomeness and her simplicity had led to a repetition of the same device for her undoing that marked the gate into the base of the heart. The bowl is roughly circular in shape. Its floor is now deep in the sea, drawn down by outhauls which pass through holes or cleats in the lower portion of the stakes which carry the sides of the net. The fish, swimming freely round the bowl at her pleasure, found the way clear and the gate open. But, alas, it also was so incised or let into the roundness of the bowl that whenever she drew near it the re-entrant angle shunted her silly head to seaward again, and she did not often turn the sharp corner that kept her from the gate. Indeed she parodied Omar, swimming

about it and about, but nevermore
Came out by that same door wherein she went.

This was the 'pound' of the 'Seventies and 'Eighties of last
century, and the reader will remember that the larger
companies sometimes set two or three in line until the
whole trap reached far into the Sound.

Let us see what the thing looked like at close quarters
and in the height of the season. The late spring weather
has turned from the chill of early May to the promise of
June warmth. For a day or two mild southwest breezes
have been blowing. The moon is entering its last quarter
and the tides are as mild as the breeze. The detestable
and heartily detested jellyfish (*Medusae*), which often
strain and sometimes break nets or even the pound poles,
are not in embarrassing evidence. In short it is 'shad-
weather,' and the fishermen are complaisant to company.
You must think of yourself as seated in the stern sheets of
the big and odoriferous sharpie. An early breeze comes off
the land; so the large spritsail is set, a little centreboard is
given her, and we move in a broad reach toward the first
bowl to be hauled, the smaller sharpie also under sail in
company.

On arrival, the small boat goes round the outer circle
of the bowl, casting off the outhauls by which the floor of
netting is kept near the bottom. The bigger craft then
enters the bowl itself by the gate which admitted the fish.
After entrance the two long 'apron-poles,' one on either
side of this gate, are pulled up from the bottom, bringing
a section of the net with them, and the gate is closed. The
floor has been released by the slacking of the outhauls and
can be raised in one corner. This is soon done, and after
being brought out of water so that the fish are driven forward it is dropped under the boat again, care being always

taken to maintain a barrier of raised net to keep the fish in front from cutting back into the overhauled portion of the bowl.

As the bowl narrows an increasing commotion is apparent. The quick gleam of silver sides gives assurance that the morning will have something to show for itself. Darker forms, some large and active, some smaller and more resigned to fate, begin to appear. The free space diminishes. Now it is so small that the water begins to fly and we can see that the catch is not only considerable but varied. Anxious eyes make sure that in this crowded corner there is no rift in the net, for I have seen the whole catch of a successful morning threatened by the rupture of a half-dozen meshes, through which as from a funnel the fish began to pour as they were crowded toward it.

Finally the catch is cornered, and through the spray encompassing the fishermen you will see the shad coming aboard in scoop nets wielded by stout arms. At last, when these and the bigger fish of less or no value are in the boat, the pocket of net is lifted by main strength and its remaining contents dumped aboard. If the uninitiated asks why this was not done at first, he has to be reminded that the total catch, good and bad, may well weigh a ton or two, that no adequate tackle for such a lift is provided, and if it were the strain upon the net would involve a risk too high to take. For he who has gone out expecting shad and nothing more is in the way of great enlightenment. The gill net with its quiet drift might have met his expectations. The hauling seine would have landed shad principally if not exclusively. But the impounded fish this morning may not supply one half their weight in shad. For here are a half-dozen blackfish or tautog, with the thick lips that give the name of *Labroid* to their family, and they would be accompanied by a host of their cousins, the cunners, if the mesh were not too coarse to confine them. It would not be surprising to find a chiquit or weak-fish in the lot, and be reminded by the fishermen that if you want him at his best he should be cooked by midday.

At long intervals a true salmon used to appear, belated scion of a house that once called these waters home. He is legally supposed to be released as soon as caught, but generally appears to have suffered such injury before capture that release was inexpedient and wasteful. The sturgeon too was once an occasional occupant of the bowl, though not very welcome if she were of large size because of the damage she could do to the net, and the lack of any active market for 'Albany beef,' as her flesh was called. Curiously enough, no one by the shore in those days seemed to consider the female's roe or, for that matter, the roe of any fish as worth eating; though of course the roe shad found a better market than the buck.

Dog-fish were common, and sharks occasional. Once, on a day's visit to one of the smaller pounds, I helped land a shark that required all the strength of two young and lusty men to drag him up the beach, though his conquest in the water had not been difficult owing to the fact that he had been so entangled in the net as to be practically 'drowned.' Once, too, years before the time of which I speak, a shoal of sharks were caught in Oyster River Bay, probably by a very long hauling seine. Two ox-carts were needed to bring them up the beach and, large and small, they numbered twenty-eight or more. The two ox-carts are to be vouched for; the number of the fish may have been thirty-eight; indeed my memory inclines to it; but for the sake of timid bathers and general credibility we will assume the lesser number. Though I have seen many large and beautiful sharks, I never knew a bather to be molested in our waters. Once I knew a seal to be caught while poaching in a pound, though he had to be shot before final capture. Now and then, too, a striped bass appeared, and codfish were not uncommon.

But the so-called 'foul fish' are as interesting as the food fish; indeed the distinction is in large degree a false one, because in the interval between then and now vast quantities of fish that once went into the scrap-heap and were sold at ten cents a tub for fertilizer have become valuable articles of food. This is particularly true of the *Heterosomata*, or general family of the flat-fishes. Here, for instance, is the northern flounder, whose white and toothsome flesh the town-dweller knows best as filet of sole — though other fish too frequently contribute to that excellent item on the bill of fare — and here beside him are a group of his small-mouthed cousins known to the fishermen of those days simply as 'flat-fish.' These are all alike in having white bellies and dark brown backs, the latter sometimes mottled as in the pretty little 'Irishmen.'

All are alike, too, in having the two eyes on the upper surface of their foolish faces. When spawned these fish swim as the shad does and have an eye on each side; but as they develop their flat-fish habit, with a white underside toward the ground and a brown protective colour on the upper, one eye begins a short journey over the head until it joins its neighbour and both look toward the surface. It is an odd freak of nature, and the landsman is often disposed to be a little incredulous of it; but the fisherman has observation, science, and a good many learned discussions on his side. The secret of the thing is, I suppose, that in the change from an 'upright' to a 'flat' habit what may be called the 'plane of change' runs below the second eye, and its habitat is by development thrust to the upper side of the fish. The flounders have biting mouths well furnished with teeth; while the flatfish have rounded mouths that seem better adapted to sucking than to biting; yet they too can take a hook, and one of considerable size, as the tautog fisherman will testify.

But the amazing thing about both flounder and flatfish in the heyday of pound fishing was the small account made of their excellent flesh. A few of the largest were shipped, to find a market of doubtful remuneration. Some were given to children of poor families who waited with their baskets for the boats to come in — baskets that never went away empty. But much and sometimes most of this admirable food went into the pile of waste. So did all the rays or 'skates,' which were edible but not marketable except among the foreign-born of the larger cities.

Two other members of the mob deserve our notice. One is *Spheroides maculatus*, a quite undistinguished little fish as he swims about the narrow confines of the bowl, perhaps six or eight inches in length to the base of the tail, brown or grey above, beautifully cream-coloured below, with an undulating band of yellow between, a blunt nose, two distinct nostrils, brilliant blue-green eyes, and a habit when free of pushing his rather slow way about the bottom, now half-burying himself in the sand and again rallying with a group of his neighbours to attack a solitary crab. Some of his cousins are far worse than ticklish to handle, so covered with spines are they; but this fellow has none long enough to trouble the hand that holds him gently.

No sooner is he held, however, than the marvel which gives him his name begins. With convulsive movements of his solemn little face he begins to swallow air; as he swallows he swells; until directly instead of a rather clumsy but distinctly elongated fish you hold a funny globe the lower surfaces of which have rounded out from a sac in the gullet as air has been swallowed and retained until one wonders when the bursting-point will be reached. His capacity for distention is such that a fish measuring about eight inches to the base of the tail has been estimated to be large enough to hold forty fluid ounces when 'blown up.' Throw him over the side, and after floating football-like for a moment the distended gullet will discharge its load, and once more a modest and rather humble little citizen will go about his business in the sea as though unconscious of ever having posed as a public figure.

But for the moment a public figure he is sure to be when he comes into the blackfisherman's boat, especially if there be landsmen present. When he puffs himself up and the mouth sinks into the middle of the resultant globe with the bright eyes above it shining in the sunlight, the small but broad incisors take on something of the aspect of the teeth of the Jabberwock in Tenniel's immortal drawing. They are set however in a face as mild and fatuous as that of the White Knight; and so arrayed in his self-important innocence, *S. maculatus* would charm the veriest cynic.

Much has been written as to the reason of this strange behaviour, but it is almost certainly dictated by the instinct of self-preservation, since so many of the allied species are thickly covered with spines that give a porcupine effect to the creature when distended. The spines of *maculatus* are, as I have said, almost non-existent, and quite harmless; but he may think that his roundness, if not terrifying, will at least prove laughable, and that in his ensuing good-nature the fisherman will return him to the sea. If so his mild strategy has its reward, for this is precisely what I have myself done time and time again when the little fellow has bitten at my bait, swollen like a Tammany district leader in my hand, and as speedily deflated himself when out of office and remanded to his native element. Not the least notable fact about the fish is that his offspring begin to practice swelling almost as soon as born, and the tiny fry of but a few days old will assume to terrify their little world by blowing themselves up into literal fishballs the size of a garden pea.

One more captive of the morning, and our list must end. He is a strange shapeless creature perhaps three feet long and possibly twenty-five or thirty pounds in weight. The good woman whose first sight of a hippopotamus evoked the cry 'Ain't he plain!' might well repeat it now, were she here, and with an added note of wonder; for he is as brown, warty, and clumsy as he is misshapen. My memory of him brings back a sentence from the description of the right whale in *Purchas His Pilgrimes*. 'His head is the third part of him,' says Purchas: 'his mouth (O! Hellish wide!) sixteene feet in the opening; and yet out of that belly of Hell yielding much to the ornaments of our womene's backs.'

To be sure, *Lophius piscatorius* has no sixteen-foot mouth, nor does any part of him so far as I know go to the corsetting of woman. But his mouth is as big as his queer body at its biggest end has room for, and the rest of him is belly. Indeed the body seems to be little more than a vast sack open at the mouth-end and tapering to the tail. The mouth itself with its enormous opening, its fringe of sharp inward-curving teeth, its expression as though the Cheshire Cat had sold herself to Satan and turned her pleasant grin to evil purpose, is a memorable sight. Nor does it belie the nature of its owner, who is a voracious and omnivorous feeder. All seems grist that comes to that eager mill, and on one occasion a goosefish, as he is commonly called, was captured off our shore which proved to contain an alewife (a herring that sometimes reaches a length of twelve or fourteen inches) and an oldwife (the long-tailed sea-duck) — a righteous judgement, as my Grandfather declared, upon his bigamy.

But how, the reader may ask, could so clumsy a creature capture so lively a fish and so strong a bird? Probably as you and I go fishing. For the secondary name of the fish, *piscatorius*, sets forth its claim to membership in Isaak Walton's family; it is scientifically known as the 'Angler'; and examination will reveal that the first dorsal ray is not only much elongated but bears at its tip a little bait-like tab which can be gently waved above the cavernous mouth; and although *Lophius* has perhaps never been caught at it, there seems little doubt that thus the mouth is filled. Incidentally he is a fish of very wide distribution, found on both sides of the Atlantic, appearing on our coast from the Gulf of St. Lawrence to Cape Hatteras, and on the other coast reaching in deep water to the Cape of Good Hope.

Now that our Farmer-Fisherman has his catch, what next? The fish were taken ashore to the door of the fish-house if the tide were high; to the edge of the sand-flats if it were low, thence to be sent ashore by horse or ox team. Then as in Scripture days the good were put into vessels and the bad cast away. The vessels were stout boxes with hinged tops wherein the fish were packed in ice to be shipped by night steamer to New York, whence the boxes were duly returned. The bad, I am sorry to confess, were simply thrown into a heap too near the fish-house, where they soon fell victims to odoriferous decay unless speedily carted off to be spread and buried among the growing Indian corn, for which they have been a specific food since aboriginal days. Sometimes they were stacked and covered with loam, to be used later after the earth had become impregnated with their virtue. In either case the procedure seems highly unsanitary from our modern point of view, although in fact I never knew any illness to be traced to it, so far from houses were the fisheries and so fresh and constant were the breezes; but such neglect at first and such subsequent use of foul fish must have bred multitudes of flies that may eventually have become carriers of infection.

Such was a typical day of the Farmer-Fisherman in good weather and at the height of the season. The crew, if the company were small, might comprise only three; or, as in the case of those to whom the reader has just been introduced, it might rise to five. Of these, one or two would probably represent part-proprietors who had some capital invested in equipment or in fishery rights. These were the farmer-fishermen *par excellence*. The others were employees, although their wage, like that of the whaleman, probably consisted of a 'lay' or share of the season's profits.

Yet these too have a right to the compound name though they may not own a rod of land; for the majority of them when fishing ceases will turn to the farms, where they find employment as labourers. Indeed, when of industrious and temperate habit they made excellent workmen, because the fisherman like the sailor was almost of necessity a handy man, ready and ingenious in all matters that required carpentry, painting, or rigging, as

well as a good mower and reaper. He never grew affluent
by fishing; but there was always a sporting chance that
a good season might give him more than average day's
wages; the taste of the sea was good in his mouth; and it
smacked of mild adventure in late March or early April
to make up a bed-roll, pack a few clothes and cooking
utensils, and drive to the 'fish-place.' The whole thing
was a sort of holiday, laborious to be sure, and sometimes
so disappointing that the fisherman would be heard to
vow that this was his last season, only to return again to
the old place and ways, as true fishermen always will.

The one or two men who were partners in the fishing
company as well as active fishermen were almost always
farmers in a small way. The large farm is a jealous mistress
or a tyrannous servant, and cannot well be left during the
crucial weeks of spring and early summer; and even the
small farmer, unless he had a father at home whose fishing
days were past or a son whose were to come, was often
put to it to plow, plant, and cultivate even a few acres.

It used to be said of one man whom I well remember in
his extreme old age that he would walk to the Ferry toward evening — a matter of two or three miles — fish
through the night, walk home toward morning, and then
put in a considerable day on his farm. Only an iron constitution, a strictly temperate habit in everything but
work, and a mind ambitious for things of abiding worth
could have kept such a man going; and it was characteristic of him that of his two sons one should have become
a clergyman of considerable repute in his branch of the
church, while the other should have followed in his
father's footsteps as a farmer-fisherman with varied
knowledge of forest, field, and sea, a ready hand for
setting a pound, building a boat, guiding a plow or wield-

ing a scythe, a well-ordered family, and the hearty respect of his community.

Sometimes such men as this son to whom I have just referred went beyond their home fishing grounds and caught more than fish. A group of them at one time were accustomed to go to the Sackett's Harbour region of Lake Ontario. They could command some capital, the lake whitefish were reasonably plentiful, and the local methods of their capture were less advanced than those upon our coast; moreover they could thus make two fishing seasons. For some time, while these men remained unmarried, the plan worked well. The difficulty seemed to lie in the fact that one could not go into the Sackett's Harbour region year after year and long remain unmarried. One by one the bachelors fell victims to the charms of Lake Ontario maidens, whom they brought back to help them set up homes. The responsibilities of family life, added to the quickness of the lake fishermen in adapting what was best in the Long Island Sound methods, put an end to this chapter in interstate commerce; but the women remained.

All whom I remember, though generally mistresses of modest homes, were persons of competence and character who reflected distinct credit upon the communities whence they came; and one, a woman of much charm and not a little beauty, became the mother of three boys, the eldest of whom was the chief companion by field and sea of my elder boyhood and young manhood. We fished and shot and walked the woods together; made friends with the elderly custodian of our public library, who used, I fear, to stretch the rules a little that I might see and read the last Littell; went to church in company on Sunday nights, and on the way out stopped by the bridge near which our

boats were moored for interminable talks, beginning with
the weather and the prospects of fish or ducks, and going
on to save the country and solve the problems of the
universe. Our paths diverged, though he came to New
Haven once or twice for a week-end visit after I had gone
to Yale. Later California claimed him and we met but
once in forty years. But a grateful memory remains of a
companionship as sound, wholesome, and happy as any
youth could wish.

Here and there among these amphibians might be
found one who, while reasonably zealous in his farming
from fishing time till harvest, must needs snatch a few
days in early autumn for a run to Montauk Point —
'Montaugue' he very likely called it — for a fare of bluefish, sea bass, or even of flounders. With one such man
I used occasionally to cruise. He was good company, quiet
yet not taciturn, a competent sailor, acquainted with all
the little harbours on both shores of the Sound and with
many of the folk who lived by them. It was characteristic
of the union of sea and land in him that when the autumn
evening fell in some cove of the Long Island shore, when
the lantern was lighted and set between us on the centreboard box in our narrow cabin and my book was open
(though I was as ready to listen as to read), then no topic
proved more congenial to William than his little farm,
and particularly his steers.

It seems a homely theme, and soon ended. Yet so far
as I can remember, those young cattle never palled upon
me or were exhausted by him. The fact is that the hand-
ling of oxen, like many another rural occupation, is a
matter of considerable skill involving even mating, careful
and kindly breaking to yoke, and wise driving. William
loved it all, and so did I when he described it.

Then the talk would wander to such small adventures

as the Montauk fishery furnished; though these were not always small. One great storm I well remember through which a group of Saybrook and Lyme men ran from Montauk to the Connecticut and towed a seine boat — a storm so violent that though I was bodily in a Yale lecture room my soul was abroad in the tumult. After another storm word came back to William's home that he with a group of other Connecticut men had been lost. It was not true, but it was a solemn rumour.

I cannot detail his record of the adventure, but it turned out that a story of disaster went both ways. He finally reached his home port anxious about the effect that the story of his loss had produced, only to be met by a neighbour who inquired, 'Hev ye heerd from home?' 'No,' answered anxious William. 'Wal, the cow's fell down on your wife and stove her all to pieces!' This was staggering news for a troubled man, though I doubt if he gave it absolute credence, knowing what manner of woman his wife was; for Mrs. William was a person of extraordinary force and competence whom no ordinary cow, however unsteady on its feet, could catch at disadvantage. And so it proved. There had been an accident of some sort, but my friend found his wife practically intact instead of 'stove to pieces.' There was a reciprocal tale of adventure to tell and all ended happily.

The old-time Farmer-Fisherman is gone from the shores of southern New England. Its coast has been suburbanized and his fish-house outlawed. He himself, if he were here, would very likely be found in the more remunerative but less varied office of caretaker for 'summer people' and their homes — a needful task, but one less calculated to twist stout masculine fibre than his work and ways of old. Yet while some of us still breathe the upper air his memory will be green.

IV

A Connecticut Farmer

THE old-time Spanish chroniclers, it used to be said, liked to begin with the Creation. It gave them a good start and it dignified their country's history. So in speaking of my Farmer and his Farm, it behooves me to go back for a moment to the foundations of our habitable world. The reason is that the Farm itself went back; and that its descent from primaeval times, forces and changes gave it not only dignity and charm but such power as it possessed to sustain its owner and his family.

Connecticut, like most of its New England neighbours, is a rugged state. It has fertile land but has it only here and there. The rivers provide some alluvial meadows. A great Triassic Belt — a region of exceptional geologic interest — reaches northward from New Haven, touches and includes the valley of the Connecticut at Middletown, and so proceeds into Massachusetts, with its sandstone broken by occasional outcroppings of trap, its sandy wastes, and its fields of reddish clay and loam. Below Middletown the Connecticut breaks through the eastern bank of this Triassic Belt, and turning southeastward invades the country of the older granite and gneiss. These form the hills, many of them still rugged as hills can well be, despite the weathering of untold centuries. Their sides are covered with rather thin soil where the archaic ledges permit its lodgement, and are besprinkled with boulders which the great ice sheet long ago brought down from the north.

In roughly parallel north-and-south billows, with here and there an east-and-west range, these hills descend to the coast. The last of them often form a breastwork one or two hundred feet high looking toward the sea. Sometimes, as in Lyme, New London, and Noank, they thrust rocky spurs of somewhat lesser elevation almost into the sea itself with an effect beloved of artists; and everywhere on hillside and in valley, spread over what might otherwise be fertile field and in profusion along the shore, lie the boulders, always present except in the salt marshes and river meadows, and sometimes so dominating a district that the merest tyro knows himself to be on an ancient moraine.

As the Connecticut reaches the Sound its narrow valley broadens to east and west with marsh and low meadow; while on the Saybrook side a coastal plain extends westward as far as one can see. It is a narrow shelf of more or less fertile land lying between the last granite ridge and Long Island Sound. Varying in width from one to two miles, indented by occasional bays with their attendant salt marshes, and intersected by tide streams whose saltness is tempered by the overflow of brook or pond, this plain is generally arable, and parts of it used to be highly cultivated. Here were some of the best farms of the region, and on one of them about two and one half miles west of the Great River and three quarters of a mile north of the Sound, our Farmer had his home.

This home was ancestral. The first settler of his name

had come, a youth of about nineteen, to help establish
the military post at the mouth of the Connecticut. Within
the Fort itself he had backed Lion Gardiner in keeping
a precarious foothold against the assaults of the Pequots.
On a February day in the perilous winter of 1636–37 he
had helped to cover the retreat to the Fort of the men
sorely wounded in a surprise attack upon the little force
that sallied out to burn the tall marsh grass and reeds
which so often served as ambush; and so brisk had been
the skirmish that almost a quarter-century later Gardiner
devoted much space to it in a letter to this ancestor and
another old fellow soldier — a letter that is now a treasured
source of our knowledge of the Pequot War.

They were grim days, those of the settlement, and their
chroniclers have too often jumped to the conclusion that
grimness was the chief characteristic of the men who made
their history. This jump has been quite too confident
and nimble to hit the truth. For in the very winter of
their discontent these pioneers laughed so heartily on two
occasions when returning from discomfiting the enemy
that Gardiner recalled the laughter over four-and-twenty
years. And lest this should seem to indicate that laughter
was rare, let me add that the whole letter is replete with
humour, often whimsical and subdued, but honest humour
none the less. Now men who could laugh like that just as
the jaws of death, and death by fire and torture, bade fair
to close upon them may have been grim upon occasion —
they had to be to live — but there were likely to be rills of
laughter in their hearts; and they were likely to hand on
some capacity for mirth to their descendants. It has been
so. I have known five generations in the line of this young
soldier, from one which began in 1789 to one which may
hope to see the year 2000; and the springs of laughter,

clean, honest, generally kindly laughter, at the absurdities, the minor contradictions, and the sheer fun of life have never failed.

Soon after 1660 it seemed safe and convenient to move the two and one half miles from Fort to Farm. There the Homestead was built. From it the First Settler directed the rebuilding of the Fort-House with its fortifications in 1676, and a copy of his letter telling the authorities in Hartford that the work was done is before me as I write. There had been cause for this rebuilding, since in the year before Sir Edmund Andros had appeared off Saybrook with two armed vessels and sent a boat ashore to ask politely if there were danger to be apprehended from the Indians — King Philip's War was in its early stages — and if his forces could help. But the Saybrook folk, like some of the Trojans of old, doubted the sincerity of Grecian gifts. It was 'but a compliment,' wrote this First Farmer as he gathered the train band of which he was captain, halted certain forces from the westward, probably on the way to fight King Philip, and, reinforced by Captain Bull, entered the dismantled Fort and hoisted the King's colours. This gave Andros his choice between firing on the flag or going on to further and more memorable adventures. He went. But this Farmer's letter still remains, outlining the situation, asking for instructions, and superscribed, 'Haste, haste, post haste upon His Majesty's Special Service.'

In this first house he died at a good old age, as did his son after him. One of the numerous grandsons born there built another in 1740 after he had grown to middle age. To him a son and grandson succeeded in like manner, the son to live a long life and die in his father's house, the grandson to build anew. This last house was erected as the futile war of 1812 drew toward its close. Its frame was up when the great September Gale of 1815 swept the coast, wrecking shipping, carrying spindrift so far inland that orchards miles from shore were blasted by it on their southern sides, and generally testing such works of man as its fury could reach. But the half-built house stood the test. The mason who was dressing the brown-stone steps to the front door was called away to help capture or re-capture a vessel in the Sound. One of its crew fired and killed him, only to fall himself when the fire was returned; and another mason was necessarily called in to complete the steps. I used to peer at them in the attempt to see where one laid down his tools to die and another, reputed to be less skilful, took up the task; but the storms of nearly sixty years had played upon them then, and the line of demarcation, if ever existent, had vanished.

These three houses, though none was built upon its predecessor's exact site, stood near each other, and all on land that had never been out of the family's possession. Some of the material of the house of 1666 was wrought into the roof of 1740, and was to be seen there as late as 1890. To the house of 1815 its builder brought his bride, and in it on the 8th December, 1831, our Farmer was born. He was the youngest of five children — too young to have known his grandfather, whose life as a soldier in the French and Indian War and later as captain of a company in Washington's army on Long Island and in New York had been an adventurous one. This old soldier had come back to the ancestral home and to the customary rural tasks; though the marks and habits of army life always clung to him in some degree, if family tradition speak true. Our Farmer's father was scarcely to be called a farmer in his own right. His energetic habit had taken him to and fro among men further than his neighbours. He had established a business in Boston as an importer and dealer in cutlery and other hardware which, when it had grown to substantial albeit modest size, he turned over to his two older sons. But his strong antiquarian bent and devoted love of home brought him back from business to the general oversight of farm and mill as soon as this could well be managed; so that in the house which his youth had built he spent his age and died, while to his acres and some of his interests his youngest son succeeded, as the youngest living son had succeeded his father in every generation since the family came to Connecticut in 1636.

But the reader may object: 'You have entitled your story "A Connecticut Farmer," using a generic phrase; and you are setting the stage for a so-called "gentleman-farmer" who rarely put his own hand to the tools of farming but drove about his land and watched the toil of others.' It is not so. This man, to be sure, was a gentleman in manner and in mind as well as by descent, if by 'gentleman' is meant one who is self-respecting and respectful to his neighbours, the master of a modest but confident and mannerly address and of a mind naturally intelligent, decently educated, and as deeply interested in the ethical conduct of life as in the day's specific task. Yet at the same time he was as truly a tiller of the soil as any workman whom he hired. His faith in the old saw,

> He that by the plough would thrive
> Himself must either hold or drive

was confessed in deeds as well as words. He shrank from no task that he would ask one of his workmen to perform unless it was one in which the labourer was more skilled than he — and it must be understood that many a farm task if it is to be well done needs a trained hand. No novice can by mere main strength and stupidness effectively manage horses or cattle, sow and reap grain, or handle axe and scythe. Like the hedger and thatcher of Old England, the hired farm labourer of New England was often a skilled workman who took pride in his skill. So this Farmer was quick to admit the superior efficiency of one man with scythe or cradle and another with carpenter's tools, and gave much of his own attention to tasks done by team or machinery — tasks which increased with the years. But my point is that he worked and liked to work with his own hands upon the acres that he loved.

They were good acres, and broad as acres went in a neighbourhood where most farms were small. He owned about two hundred and fifty of them, but so many of these were pasture, woodland, or salt marsh that he had only between fifty and sixty under grass and grain; though these were sometimes supplemented by the use of near-by fields whose owners had no means of cultivating them. The grass mentioned above needs emphasis because hay was the chief cash crop sold loose from field and barn, or pressed and shipped by sea to Providence or by rail to Hartford. Rye, oats, Indian corn, potatoes, and turnips were also raised and sold; but the sale except in the case of potatoes was generally in rather small quantities; rye and corn were often called for in the form of flour and meal, while much of both grain and roots found themselves translated into milk, pork, beef, and poultry.

The bulk of the arable farm lay close at hand and compactly together stretching field after field from the homestead to the sea three quarters of a mile away and matched across a sea-lane by the ancestral acres of near and dear neighbours. They were generally level and fenced with stone which in both size and quantity testified to the patient toil of generations of owners. Thanks to blasting powder and the invention of a rather crude rock-lifter practically all the removeable boulders had been taken out, some in pieces and some entire to form a cyclopean base for the stone walls; so that except in the back of one or two fields where ledges protruded, plough, harrow, and mowing machine could have free course. There were two outlying and distant fields, both of them fruitful. A large and hilly pasture of about thirty-five acres necessitated a half-mile journey with the cows morning and night. A great and picturesque woodlot three miles distant also supplied pasture for young cattle as well as lumber and firewood for farm, home, and market. There was another pleasant pasture on a mill stream five or six miles away and a good-sized gristmill there, which the casual observer might have thought to be a substantial asset, though its story on the Farmer's books if fully recorded must have called for a debit balance and red ink. Two other woodlots at considerable distance helped to guarantee the fuel supply and to furnish marketable products.

One class of land, if land it could be called, remains for notice, and deserves it not only for its use to the farm but because in so many ways it differentiated the shore farm from its inland neighbour. This included the amphibious stretch of shoreline and the salt meadows. Over much of the former the tide flowed twice a day, while the latter, at least partially flooded by the tides of new and full moon, were completely drowned in heavy easterly weather. The acres of this littoral — and there were about forty of them — might easily seem like so much waste in the eyes of the inexperienced. Not so in those of the Farmer. They gave variety to his land, to his labour, and to such products as he used or sold; in some measure too they tempered the heat of summer and the cold of winter. The more specific of these services I shall indicate presently.

In the midst of the fields stood the hay-barn, eighty feet of it, while behind the homestead and at a decent distance were stock-barn, horse-barn, carriage-house, corn-house, smoke-house, and their attendant sheds. The furnishings of the place were therefore good, and they were kept in good order. Of horses there were commonly three; of cows three, enough only for the family supply in times when hay was the chief cash crop, but necessarily increased when this was replaced by milk. The elder days saw too a barnful of cattle, perhaps thirty of them, including the four or five pairs of working oxen with their penumbra of maturing steers, heifers, and calves. The supply of pigs was governed by the need of the family table, the milk, grain, and household scraps that could be spared to feed them, and the plan to sell two or three litters of six-week-old youngsters to folk who raised none but were able to fatten one for their own supply and for the economical disposal of the 'left-overs' of table, garden, or small farm. The 'hired man' kept a pig if he were thrifty, and often took vast pride in digging an appraising thumb into the increasing thickness of its sides as he speculated upon its weight and the toothsomeness of sparerib, bacon, and sausages. The Farmer-Fisherman of whom I speak in another chapter was almost sure to want one, since, although he might be a man of substance, the division of his time between land and sea forbade stock-raising beyond the necessary limits of freshening a cow and the setting of maternally minded hens. As to the fowls themselves, only so many were kept as could be economically fed and sheltered. These were expected to furnish eggs for kitchen, market, and table, and finally to come to the last themselves. None were sold.

Such is the frame of our picture and the setting of the stage on which our Farmer played his part. A drab picture and a sad dull part, the uninstructed reader may exclaim. I do not think so. There were, to be sure, no lurid lights, but there were some very gracious ones for eyes that were open as were this man's to the flash of the bluebird that was often to be seen on Saint Valentine's Day — an adventurer from the thickets rather than a true migrant, of course —, to the tender grey-green of the willow catkins, the delicate buffs of the vaccinium blossoms, the head of rye that almost always met the tenth of May, the varied hues of growing crops and, when Spring verged on Summer, the chocolate of the 'blackgrass' and the golden browns of the 'red-salt' in the marshes, or the changing lights in the windswept waves of tall grass and maturing grain. He rarely halted work to gaze upon these things, nor did he grow sentimental over them. But his eyes saw them as they saw the changing moods and aspects of the sea; he welcomed their coming and felt their passing with a quiet and pensive calm. Without phrasing it to himself he knew what Stephen Phillips's Marpessa meant when she spoke of working

> with the benignly falling hours
> And beautiful, slow Time.

He would have understood and welcomed Apollo's promise to her as if it had been addressed to himself;

> Thou shalt persuade the harvest and bring on
> The deeper green; or silently attend
> The fiery funeral of foliage old,
> Connive with Time serene and the good hours;

though for fear of yielding to an overplus of sentiment he was quite capable of commenting that 'beautiful, slow Time' had brought the hour for 'chores,' and that he must put poetry aside to attend upon his horses.

Suppose for sake of illustration we live with him through a day or two. A sordid and drudging day it would be if Mr. Sinclair Lewis, Mr. Anderson, or Mr. O'Neill were depicting it in novel or play. Such high employ is beyond my pen and the scope of my memories; though there were drudging tasks enough whose multiplicity might have made them sordid had the man's interests centered in the making and saving of a dollar. Let it be granted again that dollars were needful, since he had many mouths to feed and backs to clothe at home as well as among the folk he hired. But in the last resort sordidness is a matter of mind and soul — or the lack of them; and I think that the better class of New England farmers were as free from domination by the lust for getting, saving, and spending as ends in themselves as any group of men that I have known. Like this Farmer, they needed dollars and worked hard for them; they looked twice before spending lest the dollars fail to go around; and they hoped for a frugal store of them to fend off dependence in old age. But the things that they and their wives really coveted were intelligence, integrity, the right outlook upon life, and ability to estimate and choose among its values. I do not deny that 'success' and 'prosperity' were too often appraised in terms of bank accounts; but when the rewards of life were laid out for deliberate inspection none knew better than they which had abiding worth and which perished with the using. I caught such a man once in a rare moment of unreserve. His son had just rendered a public service of no great eminence and almost barren of financial return but honourable in essence if not in power to win recognition; and the father unguardedly remarked that he would rather see the boy do that than almost anything he could think of. The thing that moved him to such confession was that he saw something of essential and permanent *right* in the young man's endeavour; and its value was beyond rubies — though he was by no means the man to minimise the cash value of rubies.

V

The Farmer's Year

MEANWHILE during this diversion our Farmer
has risen. He has fed his three horses, attended
to fowls and pigs, had breakfast and followed it
by brief family prayers — for he was an honestly devout
man who felt that the humblest task was better done if
linked to the Great Scheme of Things and to its empower-
ing Spirit — and all this in time to be out with his man or
men by seven o'clock if it were April. I say 'April' because
this month opened the Farm's season, so to speak. Then
the routine of active operations began. Then the regular
hired man who lived in one of the farm tenements was
supplemented by another who worked by the month from
April through October. They have already been out in
time to milk and care for the stock.

The work of an April day if it were fair was likely to be
ploughing with both oxen and horses, or planting potatoes
as the month went on, or possibly in its early days moving
oak and hickory pound-poles to the sea for the shad fishermen, though this would naturally be work for March.
Fences were repaired in preparation for the turning out
of cows and young cattle about the tenth of May. The
barn-yards would be cleared of manure, which a thrifty
farmer never sold unless it were to some friend's garden.

Commercial fertiliser he knew and valued as a stimulant; but for his somewhat light soil he knew too that nothing could quite replace the humus-creating substance of hay and straw worked over in his barnyards. To these in May and June when corn was up would be added 'white-fish' from the fish-places, thrown broadcast amid the growing crop, then 'evened' and buried rather too lightly; and nowhere have I ever seen nobler rye than grew the next year on corn-ground fertilised with fish. In 1877, for instance, he bought 29,000 white-fish from two fishing companies at a price which his diary does not record. Later as fishing declined or the fisherman concentrated upon shad, the Farm was obliged to take the run of 'foul fish' instead. These, though cheaper, were less convenient and valuable; yet he noted that in 1880 he took 143 tubs of them from one firm at ten cents a tub. Fertiliser of whatever sort, if good for anything, is apt to be a smelly substance and fish were smelly above measure. But he was a valiant upholder of them and used to declare when to leeward of a field where fish though buried yet revealed their resting-places that he perceived 'the smell of the field that the Lord hath blessed'; for he was rich in scripture phraseology and its whimsical application to the common day.

If the weather were lowering yet not positively stormy, a team or two would probably be sent to the sea for sea-weed. Each item of this tribute of the sea was chronicled. In 1887 twenty-five loads were carted, in 1888 twenty-three, in 1889 thirty-five, and there were years when the record must have risen considerably above these figures, stormy seasons naturally yielding more than placid ones. This weed varied in composition and therefore in quality. The kelp was probably most valuable because richest in sea-chemicals. The eel-grass of the brackish creeks was less esteemed, though still worth gathering. Among the weed the delicate Irish moss was often scattered and this would occasionally be saved, bleached, and brought to the family table as blanc mange. Most of this sea-weed went directly to the sward of grass-fields that were soon to be ploughed, some of it to the pigs to be worked over in their sties, and in the autumn a few loads would very likely be given to one or two of the workmen for banking up the underpinning of draughty houses — an interesting anticipation of the later and much more extensive use of prepared sea-weeds for the insulation of house walls.

Early in May, when corn had been planted, cows were turned out to their hill pasture and young cattle to the woodlands or to the fields about the mill five or six miles away. The cows commonly 'stayed put,' and were of course brought home every evening; but the whereabouts of more distant beasts was far less certain and involved occasional visits to their pastures, sometimes to find them content, sometimes to miss them altogether, and sometimes to find unwelcome visitors among them. It was surprising to see how generally the latter were recognised at once, not of course by any brand, for none was used beyond the occasional notching of an ear in some distinctive way, but generally by their age, colour, sex, and quality, and assigned to some neighbour, who would be duly notified and asked to claim them. One's own wanderers were often found in adjoining fields or came home of their own accord if they could gain a highway. Now and then a beast would be gone long and stray far; but only on the rarest occasions would one be permanently lost.

Thus the visits to the more distant pastures in a season when things went well were rather a relaxation than a burden. They filled a portion of some broken day, and in August might yield three or four quarts of berries, in September a basket of grapes, or in October a pocketful of chestnuts; though by chestnut time a humane farmer was very likely bringing his beasts to a home pasture where cornstalks — an admirable ration when fresh and well cured — could supplement the frost-bitten grass, and whence they could speedily come home in case of heavy storms or too great cold.

Early May also brought the problem of the home garden. I think the genuine farmer rarely liked horticulture or viewed the making of a vegetable garden as other than a bothersome though needful chore. His attitude was a little like that of the wholesale merchant toward the small tradesman. In some cases he was indifferent to the fruits of his garden when they reached the table. For potatoes, corn, and beans he had the respect due to staple products and as such he ate them; but things like tomatoes, squash, carrots, beets, and spinach were uncovenanted mercies to be availed of by such as needed and cared for them. This was of course a dietetic mistake but often partially redeemed by a personal fondness for some special vegetable. In the case of our particular Farmer this was celery, to the culture of which he grudged neither time, toil, nor fertiliser; and he had abundant reward in a day when among farmers in general the plant was little known and almost never raised.

The flower beds of his wife would be made up by one of the men on some half-day when field work was not too pressing, and the lawns or yard in front and rear were mown when lowering weather permitted. If the weather declined to lower, of course grass was slower in growth; still, it needed occasional attention even then, and the time 'while the dew is on' — a well-recognised part of the summer day in farmer parlance — would be given to it; for it was a part of the family tradition that a dishevelled yard and weedy walks must not be.

With June came the lush growth of grass, grain, and weed. Trees came to full leaf — too full for their own greatest beauty, I used sometimes to think, since delicacy of form was so often dulled by solidity of mass that even a fairly open grove tended to reverse the old-time proverb as the wood obscured the trees. June's earlier weeks were largely filled with the cultivation of corn and potatoes by both machine and hoe; but by the twentieth it was time to think of haying. Its tools were looked to. Beginnings were made in orchard, stack-yard, lanes, and other nooks too contracted to make machine-work worth while. One or two extra men were added to the Farm's force — a force of which I speak elsewhere. And so hay-harvest began — too lingeringly, perhaps, until Independence Day opened the weeks of intenser activity.

Inland, no doubt it began earlier. But the shore farm, while it had a warmer autumn and a longer immunity from frost, had also a cooler and somewhat later spring than its neighbour thirty miles to the north; and the farmer by the shore would be inclined to think that while his 'June grass' was ready for cutting the crop as a whole was still 'making grass,' especially in its undergrowth; and as hay was very likely his main cash crop, weight was an object of desire. Then, too, hay was more easily made after July fourth because it was riper and had need of less sun; notwithstanding which I used to think that it would have been better to have begun with both hands, so to speak, at least a week earlier, since the grass if thoroughly cured while the juices were in it was sweeter and richer than when these had partially hardened into fibre. But then I was never quite a farmer in my own right, as even in vacation-time my work was not continuous, and was most often done with the horses and the machines empowered by them.

It was a busy time — this of English-hay harvest, all the busier because of the thoroughness with which the work was done. Here was no swift cutting in the morning and carting in the afternoon. Horses and machine went into the standing grass soon after seven o'clock to cut so much as could be handled in the afternoon and carted the next day. With a good team and sharp knives in a clear field it was pretty work to watch the ranks of herdsgrass — one of the stateliest of grasses — which held their tall heads high and unconcerned one moment, quivering convulsively the next as the shuttle motion of the knife-bar touched them, and falling in even swathes to fulfil their destiny. But if the undergrowth of clover were dense and knives clogged, if low rocks obtruded and the knife-bar had to be quickly lifted, if woodchuck holes endangered the horses' legs or a swarm of outraged bees threatened man and beast alike, there was little time or inclination for moralising upon 'the grass of the field which to-day is and tomorrow is cast into the oven.' Let it be added that on the better-kept fields rocks and woodchucks alike were rare, and that while bees might threaten I have never known them sting either horse or driver while the machine was in noisy motion, the rattle seeming either to divert or confuse them. Yet there were occasional minor tragedies; a scared snake would not be quite quick enough, or — a subject for genuine sorrow — a sitting hen-quail would be decapitated.

In three or four hours a good team would cut enough grass for a day's curing. Scythes meanwhile had mown the field's corners and edges, which lay too close to fences for the machine to reach them with safety, since ragged borders and unkempt patches of half-mown grass had no place in this man's philosophy of farming. In the afternoon the grass was raked by horse power and put up into rather small cocks. These were generally counted for the satisfaction of seeing how much had been accomplished and to estimate the number of loads to be carried the next day. Then all was left for night to do its silent work. It was most unusual for this ritual procedure to be interrupted. However ripe the grass or fair the day it was as rare for this man to let his hay be carried on the day of its cutting as to let two men pitch it on the same cart.

In the cock the wilted grass sweated and brought its moisture to the surface. The next morning so soon as the dew had dried, it was opened, spread, aired, turned over by hand or machine, and by early afternoon of a bright day was ready to be gathered into windrows and thence loaded on one of the long ox-drawn carts. Horses were also used, and now and then two ox-carts and one large double horse-wagon might have been seen loading at the same time. But the ox-teams represented the characteristic practice in fields reasonably near the barns, and I have never seen larger or more beautiful loads of hay than those carried by oxen from them. And here I must justify my earlier statements as to the demand for skill in farm labour and the fact that two men were very rarely permitted to 'pitch on.' The tyro's notion seems to be that loading hay consists in its helter-skelter elevation to the cart by one or two men while another on the load pokes it about as best he can. It is sometimes so and it is a lamentable sight. It was not so here.

This Farmer had two men among his haymakers who are still memorable to me for their skill in loading and unloading hay. Both had followed the sea — that university of handy men. One, who came out of the navy and deep-sea merchantmen, was quick, nervous, alert, thin, excitable. With his tuft of chin-whisker, though it was short instead of long, he might have passed for a modified Uncle Sam; yet he was an Englishman. The other was a large-framed, slow, phlegmatic man who had served on coasting vessels and in fishing boats. On Sundays when dressed for church in blue clothes and with a square-knotted neckcloth that bespoke the sailor he might have sat for the portrait of Masterman Ready or such a Cornish boatman as I once saw at his cottage door on a Sunday afternoon near Land's End. Yet this man was a Yankee of Yankees with generations of Connecticut blood, some of it distinguished, in his family. So our conventional notions of national characteristics betray us.

No helter-skelter procedure for such men as these. The hay came to them rapidly but in moderate 'forkfuls.' Each came to the part of the long cart where the loader stood. Each was skilfully trimmed and quickly thrust into its appointed place in a rank of such parcels on each side of the cart while another running down the middle bound the side ranks. So the load rose tier on tier, a little more slowly perhaps than if two men were pitching on; but ah, the difference in symmetry, in height, in stability, and in an ease and quickness of unloading which abundantly compensated for any time given to care in loading. The man who fancies that farm labour is within any strong man's easy reach should try his hand once at doing what these men habitually did. It is probable that he could not get two thirds of their load upon a cart; that if he did it would not stay there until the barn was reached; or if it survived the journey that the loader could not pitch it to the mow in less than twice the time that these men took.

This was merchantable hay, most of it of the highest quality, and the Farmer's diary tells into which bay of his large barns the produce of each field went. In 1889, for instance, sixty-nine loads were packed into four bays of his eighty-foot barn; while eighteen loads more, some of it of a quality not quite so good, went to the home barns for horses and cattle. This would seem like scant provision for the stock already mentioned; but the story of haying is not yet fully told. It has indeed already been interrupted by the harvesting of rye and oats. The rye raised on these shore farms was as good as I have ever seen, especially in respect of its straw; and as the straw, pressed and shipped to Hartford, was sometimes more marketable and more valuable than the grain, this noble crop, beautiful alike in the greenness of late May and in its July gold, was worth the harvester's best care. It was reaped by machine or cradle in July and always put into the barn. I never knew it to be stacked. That would mean too much loss of brightness and possibly of weight. In August it would be threshed, its grain stored in the corn-house to be ground into flour for the table or feed for the stock and the straw pressed for market. The bays of the stock-barn would thus be cleared for the later haying to be mentioned presently. Rye was but a secondary crop however and in 1888 yielded no more than 192½ bushels from 3773 sheaves. It was like this man thus to count his sheaves, and dividing by 15 to record the 251 'shock' and 8 sheaves to which they came; and it is worth putting down here if only for linguistic reasons, since 'shock' and perhaps 'sheaf' are now almost unknown words to multitudes of English-speaking folk.[1]

If crops were graded oats would have taken no more than third place. On ground fertilised with fish the previous year they would often grow too rank and lodge so badly that considerable portions had to be laboriously cut with scythes and cured as hay. They also had a bad reputation, whether deserved or not I could never quite determine, for exhausting the soil on which they grew. For the horses *au naturel* or ground with other grain they held their place of course and half unwillingly our Farmer planted a small field of them, harvesting, in 1888, 63 bushels from 68 shock and 2 sheaves. In 1887, 66 bushels were measured and recorded as coming from 48 shock, so that the grain was more abundant or else someone bound bigger sheaves.

By the 25th of July in a good year English hay, rye, and perhaps oats were safely in the barns; buckwheat — a small plot of it — was growing and turnips were up and very likely clamoring to be thinned. What might be called a secondary haying now began. 'Edges' were cut and gathered. These comprised the borders between upland and salt marsh where varied grasses that were less than herdsgrass and rather better than blackgrass grew. Cut at the right season and well cured they made excellent fodder and were sent to horse-barn or stock-barn.

The meadow haying followed. But it must be remem-

[1] In 1887 he got but 113 bushels from 257 shock harvested — a discrepancy to be explained probably by the fact that someone bound very small sheaves; or that some straw was sold unthreshed as was sometimes done; or that the berry of the grain shriveled owing to a bad growing season. In 1878 he threshed 167 bushels from 251 shock.

bered that in the parlance of the seaside farmer 'meadow' meant salt marsh. This does not necessarily imply a tract so swampy that the foot sinks at every step. No, the greater part of this Farmer's salt-marsh acres were well ditched and firm enough to be mown in a fairly dry season by horse machine, though the horses needed to wear wooden clogs or 'meadow shoes.' These were awkward things and sometimes troublesome to keep in place, but readily accepted by good-tempered horses and perfectly practicable. Even the big haycarts were sometimes driven on well drained marshland with a high sled under the axle so arranged that the load as it increased distributed its weight between the wheels and the broad runners of the sled. The grass could thus be cured where it grew and borne directly from meadow to barn or stack.

But it was not always so. Often the green grass had to be carried to the upland. This was done by two men who bore it on poles haycock by haycock or by a horse wearing his clogs and dragging a low sled. It was wet and often weary work; for at their dryest the meadows were damp, while green grass was heavy and mosquitos thick. Once 'ashore,' as the workmen used to say, this grass was spread and cured as English grass had been. It took longer because the grass was salt, while August dews fell earlier and often remained later than July's. There were two outlying meadows, one three miles away near the Connecticut River and the other across two creeks. From the first and sometimes from the second hay was brought in a scow to some point on the mainland whence it could be carted. It is a fair question whether this was ever a sound economic practice. The distance, the time consumed by workmen in going to and fro, the slow process of loading and unloading, first the scow and then the carts, raised the cost of harvest to a high figure. But systematic and intelligent as the Farmer was, I doubt if he ever put the matter to himself in black and white — not to say red. Much of this hay when well made was of high quality; for years it had been gathered in this way; and he kept up the practice into other years when the product probably did not pay the wages of his men.

During this work Daboll's Almanac was always at hand that the phases of the moon might be kept in mind. 'What!' the reader may exclaim; 'do you mean to say that a man of this general quality, as intelligent, well educated and experienced as you make him out to be, was influenced in his going out and coming in by the waxing or waning of the moon?' Precisely so — and the influence was as scientifically justified as any shipmaster's observation. For the firmness of the meadow underfoot, his ability to do an uninterrupted day's work upon it, the question of curing grass where it was cut or laboriously bringing it 'ashore' hinged in great measure on the tides. If these were slack neap tides work could go forward promptly with a minimum of exertion. But when the new and full moon came, especially if these chanced nearly to coincide with perigee when the moon is nearest to the earth, then at high water the ditches were bound to overflow their banks; and should an easterly wind cap this climax the whole meadow might become a sea and the mown grass go sailing off upon it.

So uncertain were weather and the height of tides in August and September, and so valuable was good 'meadow hay,' that efforts had been made by the Farmer and his father with neighbours who owned adjoining lands to dyke in considerable areas, and by means of gates where a creek passed through them to control the inflow of the

tides. For a considerable time this endeavour was successful and attended with two happy results. The exclusion
of the tide even though partial enabled work to go on
through spring tides and neap tides alike, at perigee nearly
as well as at apogee, and on ground dry enough to preclude
the necessity of carrying the grass 'ashore' for curing.
Furthermore the meadow itself as it was freed from overflow tended to produce a better grade of grass; sedge gave
place to red-salt and red-salt to blackgrass.

The men who toiled upon these meadows were too much
occupied with exacting labour and often too hot, wet, and
muddy to meditate upon their beauties. Yet there was
beauty there and many a man who never owned it to
himself felt something of the pleasure of working by the
sea and with the grass that depended on it. The blackgrass
was, I suppose, the *Juncus Gerardi*, a thick chocolate-
brown grass that reached a foot in height in a good season
and sometimes lodged so as to be difficult to cut. By a
good season I mean one with plentiful rain, for these salt-
marsh growths were helped by rain as really as their upland neighbours. This was the most valuable forage plant
of the salt-meadow. Next came the red-salt, whose
botanical name I do not know, a true salt-grass ranging in
colour from the most delicate buff to a bright red-gold and
forming a happy complement to the rich sobriety of its
blackgrass neighbour. In the lower spots which were not
scalded by undrained sea-water was the green sedge, a true
amphibian about whose roots the tide came twice a day.
Yet this is only half the story told by salt-meadows to
the discerning eye; for there are flowers there too, most
memorable among them the shrublike marsh rosemary —
Statice Limonium — branching like a miniature tree and
laden with little lavender bells which retain much of their

beauty through the winter if the plant be cut and dried at the right season. Near-by in some less favoured spot which would very likely be naked but for its presence grows the leafless, upstanding — but never standing up very far — *Salicornia* or marsh-samphire commonly known as 'mutton-sass.' It is a fleshy, strongly branched little plant whose candelabrum habit suggests in miniature the mighty cacti of Arizona. Books imply that it makes good pickles for man and fodder for cattle. The pickles I have never tried, nor do cattle favour it as forage though sheep are said to condescend so far as to provide its common name. It is not harvested nor would it merit mention here but for its unusual form and its habit of changing its undistinguished green as the season ripens into the most brilliant crimson and scarlet. There was never enough of it to affect the general landscape and farmers were thankful; yet the lover of colour who found a patch in the perfection of its September splendour might well feel an uplift as real as Wordsworth's in presence of his daffodils.

This story of the haying, primary and secondary, may seem to be a long one; but it is worth telling because it filled so large a space in the Farmer's year, was so important to his livelihood, and because its day is so nearly done. Shore farming in southern New England has well-nigh ceased. Building 'projects,' summer estates, and golf links have filled the old-time hayfields with an alien throng as the country has become suburbanised. Some of these people are the sons and daughters of former owners who come back for old sake's sake; but more are strangers to the land, the sea, and the ancient ways of those who won their living from them; while not a few are literally alien in birth, speech, and habit. Even the salt-meadow is suffering a change as the ever-present dredge cuts a channel here or digs a harbour there and sometimes carries the products of its digging to raise the marsh to upland levels that houses may be built upon it. Here is, I suppose, no cause for mourning or regret. It is well that so many may be released from the dust and heat of cities to find refreshment by the sea. But some who once saw their wide old-time spaces unencumbered by the works of man except for a few busy summer weeks will look a little wistfully upon them still, and wish to have their story told while those who remember yet remain.

What came of all this labour? In answer to that question I refer again to the year 1888 as representing fairly well a time when the older type of farm procedure was still in force, though change impended. While hay continued to be the chief crop, less was pressed for a distant market and more was sold from field or mow for local use. Oxen were still employed, and the well-matched, well-trained, well-kept deep-red Devons had not ceased to be a joy to such as love the contemplative bovine tribe. I had no skill with them myself, having always ridden, driven, and handled horses, so that my prejudice might seem to be against horned cattle. On the contrary I loved and still love to see them, and always have resented the formal and half cant reference to their 'slow and patient' ways. Old oxen are slow and seem patient, but the man who could effectively handle a team of four-year-old Devon oxen had a power at his disposal which anyone might envy and all instructed men must respect — and a team moreover which if it ever got out of hand could develop a speed that put the traditional notion of their slowness to confusion. Horses were plentiful, the threat of the internal combustion engine against them being some ten years below the horizon. Milch cows were probably on the increase and dairy herds growing with the growth of urban and suburban population. So that hay was in demand though the demand was weakening owing to the increase of imports from the West and the general change about to pass upon country life in general as we in southern Connecticut knew and loved it.

But to return to my question and its answer. In 1888 this secondary hay harvest brought our Farmer thirty-two loads of 'edges' and 'meadow hay,' carrying the total for the year to just one hundred loads of all kinds. Of cornstalks cured for winter use there were nine loads beside what had been fed in autumn pastures. His potatoes made a total of 286 bushels of merchantable size and 63 bushels too small for market but still valuable for stock or fowls. Of rye, as has already been noted, there were 192½ bushels and of oats 63. Ten loads of pumpkins had been gathered and eight barrels of apples stored. Indian corn measured 440 bushels of large ears and 51 of small or defective ears. Of turnips there were 104 bushels large with 14 small and of the merchantable size 91 bushels seem to have been sold. Twenty-seven loads of wood were brought to the homestead and sixteen delivered elsewhere. A pleasant house was built this year at the sea designed mainly for a day's picnic and bathing but commodious enough for camping out in comfortable fashion. It was made to pay a modest interest on the capital tied up in it by being let to neighbours for certain days in the week.

These statistics dull as they must seem to many are really vital. To the instructed they speak of the variety and diversity of a farmer's products, experience, and skill. They may well raise the question as to how, out of these returns of his fields, this particular Farmer could pay his wages, taxes, bills for fertiliser, repairs, and renewals of machines or buildings, and have anything left for the support of his family and the education of his children. It was a pressing question because his family was large and both he and his wife, well educated themselves, were covetous of yet better advantages for their boys and girls. The measure of their achievement though doubtless short of their desire remains a wonder to those who knew them best. Both had inherited a little invested and moderately remunerative capital, which despite its narrow limits was of great help. The living won directly from the farm was of course a matter of first importance. There were some other rivulets of income which in the aggregate made a modest but appreciable stream; as for instance the earnings of the teams employed in road improvement which was just beginning to be systematic and effective. Some standing timber was sold from time to time, though this represented in a measure a depletion of capital. On the other hand the firewood marketed and used might fairly be called a crop because it did not exceed the normal increase of the farm's woodland.

It needs to be remembered too that some items of expenditure seem astonishingly low as measured by the standards of today. The family's use of ice for instance was fairly liberal. Yet there is a record of agreement with a neighbour who engaged to furnish ice for the season of 1888 at a price not to exceed fourteen dollars. Taxes were low, indeed beautifully low in rate, but bore with such disproportionate severity upon real estate as to constitute a burden. Repairs, except such as required a forge, could usually be made by one of the workmen in lowering weather or between the more exacting farm tasks. This Farmer kept an account of the cost of painting the small cottage built this year at the sea and reduced it by use of his own help to $17.51, probably less than half what he would have paid had regular painters been employed; while the work was efficiently done. Indeed he often had among his men one or two who were competent journeymen painters and carpenters. They liked some aspects of farm work; they profited by the steadiness of its employment; and they sometimes gained enough from the gardens of farm tenements and from the incidental overflow of farm products to make it worth their while.

But if someone presses the question of profit in the sense of increment to capital, the answer must be that our Farmer made none. He might have laid by something in good years either in the form of bank deposits or added acres had his family been small or his habit penurious. Instead his family was large and, as has been said, he desired the best things for his children. Moreover while he was earnestly desirous of dollars enough for the prompt discharge of all obligations to others, for decent and cleanly surroundings as well as for some gifts to religious and benevolent objects I doubt if he ever expected to enhance his small estate. It never was enhanced. During the greater part of his most active years the demands were so heavy as to absorb income and probably make some inroads into capital; and by the time his children became self-supporting the tide had so strongly turned against profitable farming that little more than a living could be made from it.

But this is not to hold him up for a moment to the reader's commiseration. He had a reward which in the scale of abiding values was a rich one. He followed with intelligence and skill a calling which he liked, respected, and knew to be constructive. Though circumstances furnished enough contradiction to make him, like most men, sometimes sorry for himself he lived for ninety years in friendly peace with God, man, and the forces of nature with which he wrought. He had admirable health. He had eyes to see the changes and beauties of the seasons as well as to note the characteristics of bird, beast, and plant, wild or tamed to his uses. He had in considerable though not in perfect measure ability to keep in mind the frequent compensations of vicissitude. If the heat were oppressive it at least encouraged the growing corn; and if an easterly storm interrupted his work it also brought him seaweed. He found enjoyment in the variety of his labour on the one hand, and on the other in the peaceful monotony of such things as husking corn in the field on pleasant autumn days or in one of the barns on stormy ones. In short, it was a sound life, not idyllic in any sentimental Fragonard-shepherdess fashion, and fraught with little worldly profit — but wholesome none the less, and of the sort that leaves a clean taste on the palate of memory.

VI

The Farmer's Avocations

IN her recent story of a Maine farm the author with an understanding heart, a keen eye, and firm hand has pictured the light and shadow of country life 'As the Earth Turns.' Both title and treatment are happy. The folk she introduces to us are real people — such folk as one finds today in any agricultural community, some cheerfully competent, some slack and complaining, some content with country life and its compensations, some eager to change it for life in town though it be lived in cramped quarters, in a mean street, supported by cheap occupation and enlivened by yet cheaper amusements.

It is all true; yet it is by no means an adequate picture of New England farm life in the latter half of last century. The farmer depicted by this novel exists, has always existed and we hope may long continue, because he is an indispensable man. But it is none the less a pity that he should so generally stand for the farmer-at-large as to bring up a picture of a man whose cultural interests were almost entirely lacking, whose reading scarce went beyond a newspaper, whose knowledge of and interest in public affairs if not limited to his school district yet circled with short radius about his parish pump, who was an awkward boor in society, and who, if a caller came in mid-evening, would be found in overalls and stocking-feet before his fire. Now a man may be like this and still be of large service to the community; he may be interesting and likeable; he may be worth writing about. He is apparently the only man whom artists great and small think of depicting when they transfer what they suppose to be 'farm scenes' to sketch-book or canvas. But he is by no means a completely representative farmer; indeed, at the time of which I speak he would not have been a fairly representative farmer. I chanced to remark to my neighbour at dinner not long ago — a woman of considerable experience of both town and country life at home and abroad — upon the excellence of the public speech which I had heard in town meetings when farmers were discussing schools and roads only to be met with the exclamation 'Not farmers!' 'Yes,' I answered, 'farmers'; and went on to tell her something of the farmers I had known.

The matter of dress may seem to be a minor one; yet there is something about a man's dress more easily perceived than defined which marks the difference between self-respect and that lack of it which often also implies disrespect of others. The common notion of the farmer appears to be that he of necessity spends his days in toil involving grime and sweat and his evenings in the raiment and the atmosphere of the day, leaving personal cleanliness to the uncertain leisure of a Saturday night. No doubt there have been and still are such men. But as I think of the five or six families which we knew the best among my boyhood's nearest neighbours whose heads were farmers in a large or small way, I fail to remember more than one home where an evening caller would not have been ushered into a well-ordered living-room to find his host and hostess in decent and cleanly array. It might be plain — it was

pretty sure to be — but it was not the working array of the
day, nor was it shirt-sleeves or its feminine equivalent.
I have known few groups of people whose self-respect
was more real. It was moreover of that genuine sort that
could live quite naturally with respect for others. Nowhere have I ever seen a higher appreciation of men of
character, learning, and eminent worth. I still seem to
remember the interest with which the services of a distinguished lawyer who was one of the United States
counsel at Geneva during the arbitration of the Alabama
claims was followed in my home; and when after his return
and appointment as Chief Justice of the Supreme Court of
the United States he called one afternoon with his wife at
my Father's house — there was a connection between the
families — I am sure that he was received with a respect
as sincere as its courteous expression was unembarrassed.[1]

Nor did the life, busy as it was both in and out of the
house, lack avocation. I find, for instance, in the record
of a January day in the life of the Farmer pictured in our
last chapter that in the afternoon he attended meetings
of the Board of Relief and the Board of Education, upon
both of which he served the town for many years; that in
the evening he met his fellow-officers of the Church to
apportion certain sums to people in need; and that he
also attended a religious service. At the same time he was
engaged with one or two members of his family in an
endeavour to secure the comfort of an old and worthy but

[1] I was called in from some small-boy occupation to be presented to the
great man, and thus began an acquaintance with the personnel of the Supreme
Court which was most happily enhanced when for a number of years the late
Chief Justice and Mrs. White became our next neighbours during the Court's
vacations. The combination of learning, humour, reverence, and unfailing
charm with which he used to expound the Constitution in our summer evening
talks is an undying memory.

dependent woman one of whose sons had many years before left the farm's employ for the army in the Civil War.
This man had proved himself to be an excellent soldier,
had come home in safety, and had since died. The mother
was left with little beyond a few unremunerative acres
and a plain house. She was evidently entitled to a pension
under the existing law. The clamour for pensions had not
then developed into the 'racket' that it has since become
though I have to admit that this was on the way. The
effort to help her was entirely disinterested, and illustrates
rather finely the neighbourly spirit of the place and time.
Red tape of course had to be unravelled — highly necessary red tape, it should be added, since in too many
cases there was room for shady practice. A near neighbour
excellently fitted for the task helped with the requisite
appraisals and returns. The Judge of Probate cheerfully
drove out to the somewhat distant home to execute the
required papers. Finally, after much correspondence with
Washington, much attention to detail, in which his
eldest daughter took a leading part, the case was won, and
he had the satisfaction of turning over to the beneficiary
a substantial cheque, and later on the savings-bank books
representing deposits which at her request he had made as
a reserve against her advancing years and needs.

The story would be scarce worth telling as an exceptional incident. In its accidents it may have been exceptional; in its essence it was normal for a multitude of the
avocations of a busy life. Of course there was no pecuniary
profit in it. There was I hope a certain increment of
neighbourly gratification but the diary gives no hint even
of this. The man's goings to and fro are set down like
his sowing and reaping or his visits to woodlot and to mill.

The service given to schools was long continued and

I think never grudged. It was, moreover, like so much of
his public work, rendered without pay beyond a small *per
diem* allowance for a few specific duties. The district
school system was still in vogue in southern Connecticut
at the time of which I write. It was patently inadequate
to the needs of the community. This man and his wife
knew it, and both were steadfast in advocacy of a cen-
tralised system with better material equipment and a
higher measure of training for teachers. The matter was
brought directly home to them by the necessity under
which they found themselves of sending their own children
to private schools at an expense that was keenly felt; but
their advocacy was none the less disinterested in the main
because it was evident that these children must be beyond
school age before the reform could be effected.

Meanwhile they and their forward-looking neighbours
did two things: quietly but urgently they pressed the
need; and they helped to bring in specially trained teachers
to the district schools. It was instructive experience to
watch the growth of this reform in the community and its
progress through a succession of town meetings. It called
into action representatives of almost all parties that
political science has known and legislative bodies have
heard. The extreme conservative was there to affirm
that what was good enough for his father and grandfather
was still good enough for him. The prudent man of
property was there, not himself averse to progress but
fearful (and sometimes rightly, since in a good cause
expenditure is too often merely lavish) of an increase in
taxation. There were cynics who, though they may have
hesitated to say it in public, in the circle of their intimates
doubted the wisdom of too much education for the children of the poor. There, too, was the citizen who didn't

exactly know what it was all about but who none the less made some scattering remarks upon the question; and beside him the sage whose sobriety, uncertain at best, was quite unequal to the strain of town-meeting day, and who from his front bench interjected a maudlin idea or two into the discussion; who was patiently heard, moreover, so long as he kept within bounds of decent brevity; and who really helped in some degree, though quite unconsciously, to strengthen free institutions, because the humblest or the bitterest man present felt that if Sam were heard then discussion was indeed free, and every citizen had a potential voice as well as an actual vote.

Underneath it all ran the strong purpose of generous-minded men to provide better things for the future than the past had known. The current of this purpose by no means had free course. Sometimes it was obstructed, sometimes turned aside, sometimes temporarily lost amid the sands of prejudice or indifference. But it was a purpose that rarely slept, never died, and finally prevailed. Among its most steadfast champions were the clergy, the substantial farmers, and their wives.[1]

As with most matters relating to country life there has been a vast deal of piffle, some of it stupid and acrimonious and some of it stupid and sentimental, talked about the 'little red schoolhouse.' In the first place, I scarce ever saw a little red schoolhouse in southern Connecticut. With the exception of one substantial building of red

[1] Years later, after watching from the Speaker's Gallery for several consecutive days, and on two occasions the proceedings of the House of Commons, I was impressed by an almost humorous resemblance between the types of speaking gladly heard in Parliament and in town meeting. The man who found acceptance was the informed man who could marshal facts and ideas with clearness and direct them *ad rem*. The flamboyant was held in general contempt. The parallel with Congress has seemed less marked because of a congressional tendency to flatulence.

brick almost all that I knew were painted white and kept
in decent repair. The teaching that went on in them was
the victim of several untoward circumstances. For one
thing it was spasmodic. Some of the pupils might be
present for but one or two of the three terms; or, if a
pupil were in attendance throughout the year, in that
time he would probably have two and might have
three different teachers no one of whom had been trained
in the technique of teaching; and there was no systematic
grading. Under such conditions both teaching and learning were bound to be more or less scrappy. But they were
by no means so contemptible as some superior critics —
and no critics are more superior than those professional
persons who absurdly insist on calling themselves 'educa-
tors' — assume.

For one thing the pupils had the advantage of at least
part-time instruction by men. This is said with full
recognition of the need that children have of woman's
care and of the special gifts of understanding and sympathy as well as of the instinctive power of imparting
what they know that women often possess. No system of
education can be what it ought without large place in it
for the woman teacher. But none the less men are needed
in far larger measure than we recognise in our American
public school system, where a boy or girl may pass through
all the 'grades' and possibly through a considerable part
of the high school course without coming under the continued instruction of a master. In the district schools
masters were generally employed in the winter when
masculine authority was supposed to be needed on
account of the increased attendance of older boys; and
when men were engaged with this end primarily in view
they were too often worth little enough for any other

purpose. But there were a good many masters who without any special training were still able to give their pupils much and give it in a memorable and sometimes an inspiring way. I never went to a district school myself except for a few weeks in childhood when the Academy was under the cloud of an interregnum, but I have known many of their teachers and listened to the experiences of two generations of their products. It may be worth noting that one of the things that my father remembered having learned in district school and that he passed on to me in early boyhood was the logical distinction between the phrases 'the first two' and 'the two first.' His teacher was a farmer and surveyor with disciplinary methods which were open to criticism; but he knew about a good many things, he had reasons for what he knew and stated reasons for what he taught. Another farmer known to me who sometimes taught school was a man of scientific attainment in the field of ornithology and a skilled taxidermist. How much of this was utilized in his class-room I cannot say — less, one may be sure, than would be the case today; but he was a man whose knowledge, both theoretical and practical, any boy interested in the life of field, forest, and sea must have respected. While this chapter was being written I chanced to talk with a man who after getting a good part of his early education from a district school went on to Yale, took sundry degrees there, won a place on its faculty, and left to take the headmastership of an important school for boys; and it was interesting to discover that while professionally alive to the shortcomings of these district schools he was so far from being contemptuous of them as to mention with some degree of respect and regard the very man whom I had it in mind to use as an illustration of their crudest methods. It suggests a caution against our modern worship of technique.

In our Farmer's diary are set down the days in which he conscientiously visited the four district schools of the town, sometimes in conjunction with another member of the Board and sometimes perhaps with some unofficial but competent neighbour whom he hoped to interest in the betterment of conditions. It would be a far cry from his unprofessional inspectorship to that which for so many years occupied Matthew Arnold; but I am by no means certain that his modest suggestions were not as well fitted to the school's needs as any made by the famous critic. One may at least be sure that no such train of weeping teachers was left behind as marked the day when President Eliot of Harvard accompanied Mr. Arnold in his inspection of a group of London schools, only to tell him at the day's close that such criticism of teachers in presence of their pupils as he had indulged in would not be tolerated even in the least enlightened sections of rural America. 'I do not think he liked it,' was Mr. Eliot's comment. It may well have been so. Our debt to Matthew Arnold in the fields of criticism, poetry, education, and constructive religious thought is so great and as yet so grudgingly acknowledged that I dislike even to suggest his failings; but a lack of good taste and instinctive sympathy sometimes betrayed him as his 'Three Lord Shaftesburys' will long bear witness.

No real understanding of the farmers of southern Connecticut can be gained that fails to take account of the 'Academy' which so many towns boasted and which supplemented the teaching of the district schools. These academies were private institutions in so far as they usually received no support from the town beyond exemption from taxation. Though free of town control they were not managed with any view to private profit, but represented a co-operative endeavour to provide more advanced instruction than the public schools could furnish. The teachers were often young college graduates or men with whom teaching was more than a winter avocation. My Grandfather, I remember, was interested in the welfare of our local Academy, though it was then about to be taken over and superseded by a private school which was attracting local day-pupils as well as resident boarders to its classes. Our Farmer had enjoyed the academy privileges in the heyday of their influence and so had many of his neighbours. They were privileges of no mean value. The teachers to be sure were not pedagogically trained; but there is a gift of teaching which normal training cannot give, though it may either take it away or at least half smother it with a magnified technique. The advantages of 'courses in education' and normal training are not to be gainsaid; but too often they give the layman the impression of emphasising method to the serious disadvantage of matter.

In the Academy which this Farmer attended and in the private school where most of my own school days were spent, more stress was likely to be laid upon what a man knew and what he was than upon his mastery of the mere tricks of his trade. My old headmaster probably violated every rubric and canon of the normal teacher's code. But he knew a good many things; he had fearless and pronounced views, some of them doubtless prejudiced; and with it all he had character — character in the moral sense of devotion to what he thought right and in the further sense of marked and memorable individuality. He did me abiding good; and when the other day I made

some reference to him in conversation with another old
pupil who had himself become a successful teacher, it
was to find my opinion echoed and reinforced with especial
emphasis upon the lasting influence exerted by the good
man's conduct of morning and evening prayers; and here
again it was his matter as well as his manner that counted.

During one rather unhappy year this headmaster
employed a teacher from a normal school — and it was
the normal school of a state in the front rank of educational
advance. This teacher was a most worthy man, painstak-
ing, conscientious, friendly, and the master of a multitude
of educational gadgets. But, alas, that was about all. He
was so wedded to his gadgets, so dependent upon his box
of teaching tricks — though most of these were good —
that he always seemed to me to be teaching manner rather
than matter; and though scarcely fifteen at the time I
found myself a little drawn to him not so much for any
personal quality he had as because his lost condition apart
from the ways the scribes had taught him appealed to my
boyish sympathies. Let me repeat that I am by no means
decrying the worth of normal training. It is considerable.
In some cases it is doubtless great. But Methodology
always has so many dangers; modern 'psychology' has so
many long-haired and wild-eyed professors and practitioners; State Boards of Education have been so greedy of
power, so often tyrannous in its exercise, and so jealous of
variety in the character of schools; and Professors of
Education, unless they are sadly misreported by the
metropolitan press, show such eagerness each year to
overturn the accepted theories and methods of the year
before that the plain man questions whether the art of
teaching can really be so esoteric and mysterious a thing.
He admits that here as elsewhere revolution must some-

times take place and that organic evolution is to be expected and welcomed; but these learned practitioners of educational theory seem ill content with evolution or even with occasional revolution. They spin so like midges in the thin hot air of theory that the layman dizzily wonders, not merely what it is all about but whether it is about anything; and when he sees as the writer saw the other day a young man of marked ability and exceptionally wide information, the graduate of one famous university and Master of Arts of another, of proved ability moreover as a private teacher, denied a very modest position in a public school system on the ground that he lacked some particular 'hours' or 'points' in theoretical education, the wonder grows.

All this may seem like a digression. Yet it has its bearing upon the cultural side of this Farmer's life and the intellectual atmosphere of his home and neighbourhood. He had gained in district school and academy an education of no very great scholastic extent but of an essential soundness and of a sort which emphasised the judgements of a singularly fair and judicial mind. It was quite natural that he should have served so long upon the town's Board of Relief and passed upon the justice of his neighbours' tax assessments. It was natural too that his diary should recall so many appointments to appraise estates or estimate a fair division of crops and stock when landlord and tenant farmer parted company. His words in town meeting were generally few and quite unaccompanied by any gesture of the hand or emotional cadence of the voice; but they were so reasonable, clear, cogent, and fair as always to carry weight; and a State Senator whom I chanced to meet while travelling once spoke to me of the effect which they produced upon him.

He rarely aspired to any contested office. That of Selectman he did not desire; that of Representative in the State Legislature he filled for one term and may have felt some disappointment at not being summoned again; but there were always so many candidates for that eminence, some of them eager; and it did not suit him to 'run for office.' The things he did for the community were generally quiet, necessary things involving little publicity and less pay.

One thing remains to be noted; and the note is needful to a fair estimate of him or the class of farmers whom he represented. If I should picture this Farmer on a winter evening in his 'library' a shout of Homeric laughter would rise from my readers — should they be numerous enough; and Mr. Mencken, who so generally has a thumb to his nose when referring to rural America, would forthwith clap the other there; which is a pity because Mr. Mencken in his more lucid intervals does not impress one as meant by Nature to be nasty, though he has shown uncommon gifts for going beyond Nature in this respect. Yet if all the books in that comfortable house had been gathered in one room its walls might very well have seemed lined in library fashion. Like most household collections, they were a varied lot, the bad rubbing shoulders with the good. Many had been handed down from his father — Thomson's 'Seasons,' Pope's translation (or paraphrase) of the 'Iliad,' one or two of Southey's longer poems, and Sir Walter Scott's 'Tales of a Grandfather' and 'Waverley.' The novelist of course whose astigmatic eyes peer into the gloomy village home of his fancy would find no books worth mentioning except, if the Puritan tradition were maintained, a Bible, 'The Pilgrim's Progress,' a volume of Calvinistic sermons, and possibly a copy of 'The Dairyman's Daughter' as a sop to youth's longing for fiction.

Well, here there was a Bible; indeed there were several, and one, the two-volume 'Cottage Bible,' was illustrated with really excellent woodcuts or engravings; there was a fat little 'Pilgrim's Progress,' but, alas, no sermons to speak of with the exception of a volume or two by Horace Bushnell, one of the most elevated and fruitful thinkers of his day. Foxe's 'Martyrs' was missing too; but there was such a world of fine blood-curdling reading in Foxe that the children's clamour for him had finally to be gratified and he was borrowed. Shakespeare was there of course; Cowper, too, with Shelley and Tennyson; Longfellow and Whittier stood side by side, while Bryant was represented by his 'Library of Poetry and Song' which was so much used as finally to demand rebinding. Byron could be had within a hundred yards from the library of an uncle, a retired clergyman, who made his home near-by and whose books were at the family's disposal; though Dickens naturally went to and fro much more often than Byron. Wordsworth was lacking and perhaps no failure of completeness could have proved more serious had it not in some measure been made up by the Farmer's memory; for he and his mother before him had a number of the simpler poems of Wordsworth and Southey by heart and some of the children were soon letter-perfect in them. A reading book called 'The National Preceptor' used in the old Academy was partly responsible for this acquaintance with these two poets. It had indeed, like the table approved by Doctor Johnson, a deal of fine promiscuous feeding to set before the reader, some good, some bad, some difficult to classify. In this last group were specimens of N. P. Willis's blank verse which won our Farmer's heart, especially David's 'Lament over Absalom'; and

I still think of them as having not only poetic grace but cultural value despite the overestimate of Willis in his own day and some good old lady's fabled reference to Goethe as the 'N. P. Willis of Germany.'

The book cases held as might be expected a few volumes of agricultural manuals, some digests of law suited to a business man's use, two large histories of the Civil War, one popular and of little value except for its portraits and the other far more serious and reasoned; and with them the many-volumed Low's Encyclopaedia, forgotten now but full of nourishing meat. Above it reposed a black-bound D'Aubigne's 'Reformation' which even historically-minded children found too forbidding to attempt. There were too, 'Robinson Crusoe,' both parts of him, in unabridged form, revealing even to the undeveloped mind the inferiority of sequels, the 'Arabian Nights,' Guizot's 'History of France' in the unbound parts with rather striking illustrations which were then coming from the Putnams' press and De Forest's 'Indians of Connecti-cut' which if read too early in life distinctly increased the difficulty of going to bed in the dark. 'Masterman Ready' though in abridged form helped to make Marryat's name blessed and there was a liberal sprinkling of other novels old and new; for this Puritan household was as far as possible from discouraging fiction except in poisonous form or debilitating doses. Mayne Reid and Oliver Optic were permitted but not encouraged as being overwrought, improbable, and the sort of thing that one was expected to outgrow. If one wanted adventure, Irving's 'Astoria' would supply it and mediate some geography and history as well.

This list could be greatly prolonged if space or the proportions of my story permitted; as it is, only one more set of books can be mentioned. There were two quarto volumes of the 'Penny Magazine.' Nobody, I suppose, remembers now this attempt of the versatile Lord Brougham to popularise learning; and the magazine must have ceased publication long before the time of which I write. But it had left a highly rewarding residuum in the shape of these two bound volumes with their varied information and occasional illustrations among which there were some reproductions of Raphael's cartoons. I repeat my confession of faith in the progress which the instruction of youth has made along many lines. But I sometimes wonder if the boy who lay on his stomach studying Raphael's Cartoons in a book too big to be easily held and on a Sunday afternoon, in those far-off Victorian days which are now so decried and in a household where some Puritan traditions were still regarded, was after all so much worse off than his counterpart of today with his face buried in the coloured 'comics' of the Sunday newspaper or his eyes goggling at the overdone love-making of the 'movies.' Of course he had been to church, without enthusiasm perhaps but also without objection. It was a part of the Order of Nature; his parents submitted to it; they even esteemed it; and in the long run he gained a good deal of both intellectual and spiritual value from it. Pretty soon the books would be put away and he would go with his Father and Mother for a walk in the fields — almost the only opportunity which their busy lives gave for such diversion — when he might run and shout (if he did not shout too loud). No doubt it seems a sad picture to the eye of today — this combination of country life, Victorian convention, and Puritan regard for worship and some form of Sunday-keeping. I am not defending it. I am simply pointing out that it had its compensations.

Now it is one thing to have books in the house and quite another to have them in the life of the household. Here they entered the household and their introduction was one of this Farmer's chief avocations in the longer evenings and on occasional stormy afternoons. As a very young man on his way to Boston for a brief visit to his brothers he was storm-bound at a sister's house in Stonington, and one of the incidents of the visit was his reading to her Bulwer Lytton's 'Last Days of Pompeii.' He had a capital voice for such exercise, moderately deep, quietly restrained, and quite free from those patronising tricks of elocution which some people call 'expression,' but which too often are only a form of saying 'I understand this; it is doubtful if you can; but if I interpret it into dramatic terms suited to the meanest capacity it is possible you may.' He read naturally, with intelligence and with a quite characteristic conviction that his hearers possessed an intelligence equal to his own; so that he could be heard for hours on end without weariness. He fortunately married a young woman whose practical gifts were equalled by her intellectual interests. She was the eldest daughter of a physician in a near-by town who had given her excellent educational advantages which her eager mind was quick to improve.

With an interest in most books she had almost a passion for history and for the better ranges of fiction. Her hands were marvellous busy with feeding and clothing her large family; and it was like a special Providence that beside the same table and under the same big lamp there should have been so good an emissary and interpreter of the authors that she loved. Macaulay's 'England' was not among the family books; but it was in the farmhouse of near neighbours and intimate friends; and it was read.

Irving's 'Conquest of Granada' was in the village library; his many-volumed 'Life of Washington' was available in another friendly family; Guizot's 'France' in untold numbers was, as I have said, in the big bookcase; Parkman was either in the house or near-by; 'Les Misérables' was to be had by rental or on fair terms of exchange; and the John S. C. Abbott biographies, though on a lower literary level, were not to be despised. Good doses of nonsense were interspersed for seasoning. The children as they grew up had their own fare from the 'Youth's Companion' and 'St. Nicholas,' though these were not expected to take the place of real books; and many stories of the day, some good, some poor, and most of them judged pretty fairly on their merits, found place in the catalogue. In one wintry season I find two unusual entries to the effect that this busy man stayed in the house most of the afternoon and read 'Ben Hur.' I put the fact in that critics may find an adequately 'bourgeois' item on which to whet their teeth, wondering a little as to what the considered opinion of these people upon the curious and once highly popular story may have been. No doubt they liked its rather strained romance. But equally without doubt they turned from it with appetites unspoiled for books that abide.

Here the somewhat too prolonged story of this particular Farmer and his family must end except as occasional future reference to them has to be made because of the light thrown by his diaries upon the works and days of his neighbourhood. Some will think that the haze of memory has diffused too bright a glow over the picture as the half-mist of evening sometimes will; and that too much has been made of a unique situation. The reader must remember that every man and every family is unique. Classification of farmers, doctors, or sailors is not an aggregation of identities. On the contrary, the judicious student of society well knows that there is sometimes as wide variety within as between groups. The life I have striven to depict was not idyllic; nor was it in the least romantic; measured merely by monetary return it was not especially successful. Into the group of neighbours among which it was lived not only the common griefs and sorrows of life entered but on occasion grim and stark tragedy stalked; and all shared these to some degree. But none the less this life was real and it was genuinely constructive.

VII

The Hired Man

THE problem of agricultural labour has agitated society since the Israelites made bricks in Egypt and sought straw to bind their clay. Greece and Rome leaned heavily on slaves and found their service wasteful as forced labour must always be. By degrees the slave gave way to the serf, whose lot proved sometimes harder than his predecessor's. Now and then indeed the pent-up fires of misery burst their social bonds and outbreaks like those of the Gallic peasantry in Maximian's day, the Jacquerie of France in 1358, Wat Tyler's almost contemporary rebellion in England, and the Peasants' War of the early Sixteenth Century, terrible alike in its inception and in the sea of blood which drowned it, tell of sorrows bitter beyond bearing.

One of the things to be especially noted in their story is that so rarely was there anyone upon their side literate enough to describe conditions as they really were. 'Piers Ploughman,' to be sure, spoke for the poor man and what Langland makes him say needs to be remembered if only for its contrast with the sleek contentment of contemporary Chaucer. But it was not until the time of Arthur Young and the French Revolution that the country poor began to find a voice that was really audible. Sir Frederick

Eden published his famous work on the 'State of the Poor' in 1797 and printed sundry family budgets, supplied by agricultural labourers. Later Cobbett wrote his 'Rural Rides'; and Kingsley followed with suggestions of what a poor man's life in the country might become and with pictures of what it was. It ought to be added that from the socialism of Marx itself the agricultural labourer had little to hope and much to fear; since one of the few things Marx praised capitalism for was that it had at least rescued 'a considerable part of the population from the idiocy of rural life.'

Now it seems a far cry from all this to social conditions in rural New England at the time of which I write. There was no 'peasant class.' Strictly speaking there never had been a peasant class. Even the so-called 'bond-servants' whose appearance in the family tree sometimes gives pain to well-to-do and socially secure descendants may well have been the equals of their masters except for lack of funds to make the journey to the new world. Once there and the term of agreed-upon service ended, the world was their oyster, which some of them could open as well as those who brought them over. Land was not so difficult to obtain and building not so costly but that the temperate, industrious, frugal, and moderately competent man could generally have a home, a garden, and perhaps a pasture or a small farm if he would pay the price in foresight and self-control.

The small farmer who had few acres and little stock cut his working coat according to his cloth. If he had a family of sons and these were willing to live out their minority at home he could work his farm with fair efficiency. If he had daughters only he must needs turn to dairy, poultry-yard, and garden for his frugal monetary returns. One

such man I knew and greatly respected. He kept a few
cows, one horse, a comfortable bevy of fowls. His home-
acres were not many but they were conveniently disposed
about his homestead, well fenced, and reasonably fertile.
Some pasture and woodland lay at a distance. True to the
south Connecticut tradition, he also had a bit of salt
meadow on a tide stream a half-mile away.

Except for the occasional help of a boy in the crisis of
his haying or some other harvest this man worked his
small farm alone with his one horse or perhaps a pair of
young cattle. If things beyond his strength were needed
he might 'change works' with a neighbour who had teams
and machines at his disposal, thus paying in labour rather
than in money; or at husking-time he would help out for
a few days and take his pay in corn or cash as the case
might be. But generally this quiet, intelligent, hard-
working man was alone in his fields or about his barn.
His industry, integrity, genuine piety, and kindly neigh-
bourliness made up an element in my own education that
grew instead of waning with the years; and when I went
to his funeral (he died at a great age) it seemed as though
a long chapter in our neighbourhood's history had reached
its term.

It was a history which in some aspects of it he probably
knew better than any other man of the town, for he had
not only become its oldest citizen, he had in his modest
way possessed and followed the guidance of a true antiquarian instinct. His home was so near to mine that
I often saw him at his daily round and wondered whether
he ever felt the manifest limitations of his lot. If so he
gave no sign though I noted that among the hymns sung
at his funeral, hymns which he had himself chosen,
appeared the one beginning

Father, whate'er of earthly bliss
  Thy sovereign will denies
Accepted at Thy Throne of Grace
  Let this petition rise:

Give me a calm, a thankful heart,
  From every murmur free;
The blessings of Thy Grace impart,
  And make me live to Thee.

As written by Anne Steele in 1760 or altered by Toplady in 1776, those lines had probably been sung by this man's family in three or four generations. To him at least the petition had been granted.

The uninitiated may fancy that such a man must have called upon wife and daughters for some field tasks. It was not so. Today this might easily be done. Since the late War a girl in overalls on hay-rake, mowing-machine, or tractor excites little wonder. But in the Victorian time and the settled neighbourhood of which I write a woman in the field was almost unknown, and even in the kitchen-garden her work was usually confined to picking straw-berries, currants, or such vegetables as might be needed for the next meal; and in the last case it would very likely be for lack of a man or boy to meet the crisis. In her flower-garden, of course, a trowel or small hoe would fit her hand as the sunbonnet did her head. But to see full-sized implements of this sort wielded by a native-born woman in the field would have roused astonishment and even if she were evidently a foreigner of the peasant class, the fact might excite remark perhaps a little touched with pain. I once heard in a well-to-do farmer's home an echo of the inquiry by some town-bred ignoramus as to whether his daughters milked. It was cited as an illustration of

the absurd verdancy of the inquirer and for the sake of the
general humour of the idea. To be sure, women had milked
cows in the old days. Today quite possibly they may
again, or at least tend the machines that do so. But at
that time I doubt if one of the intelligent and competent
girls who were laughing at what seemed to them a ludicrous question could have named one acquaintance among
the daughters of neighbouring farmers who either did or
could milk. They would have felt almost as embarrassed
on a milking stool as in a modern bathing dress — and
very likely placed it on the wrong side of the cow.

The farmer whose fields and work were somewhat more
extensive than my good neighbour's but who still shrank
from the expense of a man hired by the month would
sometimes avail himself of a boy for whom the town
officials desired a home. He was certain to be poor and
probably an orphan — and he might also be of old and
perhaps good native stock. He might or might not be
'bound out' for the term of his minority. In fiction we
expect to see such a boy scantily clothed, poorly fed,
cruelly punished, and in general made to feel his inferiority
to the family. No doubt there were such cases; but I doubt
if they were either normal or very common. The only boy
I knew who could illustrate this favourite theme of the
novelist was one of two brothers who was placed in the
home of decent but somewhat hard-bitten people. I
doubt if he was starved, and I should hope that he was
adequately clothed; but he probably found little sympathy, and it was generally believed that he met unduly severe punishment for his occasional lapses. Of
course in novels the New England neighbourhood is quite
too busy with its own narrow and sordid interests to pay
attention to a poor boy in such case except possibly to

make him a subject of gossip. It was not so here. Kindly neighbours noticed, felt pity, took friendly action, and the boy was moved to another home. The head of this new household was a deacon in the Congregational Church, then an old man. His home and its responsibilities were shared by his son-in-law, who was from time to time a selectman of the town. Now, readers of books dealing with New England life must long ago have learned that of all men deacons and selectmen are the most callous to suffering and the most forward in grinding the faces of the poor. Yet, *mirabile dictu*, in this family where selectman reinforced deacon, the boy lived out his minority, contented and to all appearance happy, the friend of every member of it and in particular of the deacon's daughter and the selectman's wife, a woman of kind heart, cheerful nature, and abounding vigour who proved a second mother to him and called forth his loyal regard. In later years like so many boys from the farm he went to the city finding useful and stable employment there in public utility service.

The older of these boys was placed in the home of well-to-do farmer-fishermen within two miles of his brother and with them lived out his minority seemingly as contented and happy as the sons of the family themselves. Both of these sons were school-teachers as well as farmer-fishermen. The boy gained a decent education from them while he learned the ways and works of farm life. But the marine aspect of their amphibian interests had chief charm and when freedom to go his own way offered it was to the sea he turned. Yet not as a sailor. When shad-fishing was over lobstering began, and when the season advanced still further the lure of bluefish or sea-bass around Montauk Point took him there. Or the presence of little bluefish over his lobster pots, of clams and oysters along the shores of the bay, or the call of a fishing party helped to fill his long day and increase his modest store. Of steady habits and unquestioned integrity, he made his way, married a young woman as worthy of him as he of her, bought his acre or two of land, built his house, made his garden, reared and educated son and daughter, and lived to see both settled in substantial homes. His was an honest, free, independent, respectable, and respected life; never affluent to be sure, but on the other hand never in want.

The larger farmers, of course, hired men for considerable terms. The one to whom my preceding chapters are especially devoted, in the more prosperous years used always to hire one man for the full twelve months. I have known him to hire two; and there used to be one or two more from April to October. The charms of fishing sometimes interfered with this last arrangement by luring a particularly dependable man to the sea during spring and early summer; but they released him by haying-time, when he was welcomed and kept until the press of autumn work was over.

Who were these men? Originally, of course, they were of as sound New England stock as those who employed them, not infrequently the sons of neighbours who were so abundantly supplied as to be able to spare one or two from their own fields, or the children of artisans who wanted either to pay their way at home, earn something toward a higher education, or save for a little farm of their own. Others and some of the best were the sons of farm labourers who had accepted their fathers' lot for themselves, sometimes perhaps of grim necessity but not infrequently because it suited them. They did not sentimen-

talise over country life or over anything; they were quite
as likely to grumble (though with a sort of muted pride)
at its hard labour; yet on the whole they liked it, knew
their own aptitude for it and skill in doing it, felt its
variety, and were fairly content with their lot. Some of
them became attached to a certain farm until they almost
preempted a claim to its foremanship, and in an occasional
instance such a man would spend most of his working days
with one employer.

There was another class of the native-born or of
British birth — the English and Scotch, despite their
frequent delay in accepting a change in citizenship and
taking out naturalisation papers never seemed to be
foreigners in the full sense — who must be mentioned.
Some of them were among the best of workmen, intelligent,
skilled, industrious; but they drank. Here and there one
might be known as an habitual drunkard. As often he
was a man whose drinking bouts were occasional, yet
frequent enough to undermine his dependability and block
the way of his advance. Indeed I have often thought
that, when the long indictment against alcohol as a beverage is finally drawn up, one of the chief articles in it
will be, not the occasional moronic sot which it has made
or even the violent deaths which it has caused, but the
number of men of rather superior mental, social or physical gifts, whose careers have been tragically thwarted by
their occasional indulgence. Almost every New England
village known to me has had its quota of men of good
natural parts and often of education and breeding who are
there and inadequately employed simply because they
cannot hold, there or elsewhere, positions to which their
abilities would entitle them and from which their unstead-
iness bars them.

Now and then among the labourers a man took warning in time. One such, a former sailor, a capital workman in the field and competent enough in one or two trades, came face to face with the fact that he was dangerous when drunk. I can still remember the wife of a fellow workman coming in alarmed agitation to my Grandfather begging the exercise of his authority to quiet a quarrel in which this man was involved; and how Grandfather called for his boots and went promptly out into what seemed to me imminent peril. It might well have been so for he was quite too old to have used physical force though naturally a powerful man; but he had the authority of age, position, and manner. The fight was stopped though not until the sight of a bloody fist had left an ineffaceable impress upon my childish memory; and this man, who was very likely the aggressor, had a part of his lesson. On another occasion, when a brave woman whom he even when drunk did not quite dare to harm took away his shotgun with gentle violence, the lesson was emphasised. Convinced that drink literally crazed him to the extent of endangering others he stopped drinking, bought a bit of land, moved and enlarged a little house, in due time added an arable field, purchased pig and cow, and gained a place in the steady life of the community as permanent as it was useful. But in this respect he was an exception. As a rule once a drunkard always a drunkard, whether a sot or the victim of an occasional spree; and the number of competent men whose occasional sprees had tragic endings reached in the aggregate a solemnising figure. This is not the ranting of a professional prohibitionist. If it were decent and would not give needless pain to many people now living, I could be specific with names and dates leaving the reader to judge whether the list were significant or not.

It is not to be wondered at that John Barleycorn was in pronounced disrepute among the farmers of whom I write. Long practice of a profession that has brought me into close and vital contact with the problems of the well-to-do and the poor has convinced me that it is difficult to exaggerate the indictment against alcoholic beverages. They increase poverty directly. They often predispose to tuberculosis through the occasional exposure of the drinker and the undernourishment of his dependents. In many cases they weaken where they do not overthrow the mental and moral barriers against venereal disease. The recent attempts at so-called Prohibition were both ill-advised and ill-executed; but the folk who stood behind them were right in their conviction that they were aiming their shafts at Public Enemy Number One.

The cynic may ask with what consistency the employer could object to the hired man's whiskey when he himself had hard cider in his cellar. The question always assumes the cider and its hardness; and today a 'movie' that had a farmer in its cast would scarce be a 'movie' if it did not picture him as guzzling cider or tippling cider-brandy. Cider is almost as much a feature of the rural scene as painted by the ordinary news reporter as are the corncob pipe and the overalls hanging by one precarious suspender. Well, there is a certain consistency in the picture. If in my boyhood's vicinity you could have found a farmer who used overalls in the place of trousers or who smoked a corncob pipe you might at the same time have discovered an habitual hard cider drinker. In point of fact it was not often so. Cider was made in moderate quantities. It was used in very moderate quantities, though with some misgivings on the part of anxious mothers, in its practically non-alcoholic state; and the use diminished rapidly with its growth in potency. It was expected to sour and become vinegar. That was its final cause in our neighbourhood; and its use as a beverage was but a brief episode in its earliest stages. There was but one man among those whom we knew well who could be called a farmer and who also probably had too frequent and eager recourse to his cider barrel; and in his case, as careful Herodotus was always saying, I can state nothing of my own positive knowledge. I do not mean that these men were all absolute teetotalers. Some, though very few, may have made and used a little wine. But the farmer who was recognised as such in the community was in almost every case a strictly temperate man and usually a total abstainer.

The English, Scotch, and native labourers were reinforced by a wave of Irish who came in numbers with the increased emigration of the 'Famine 'Forties' and were brought into our coast towns by the railway building of the early 'Fifties. To them succeeded a lesser wave of Scandinavians, generally Swedes, who came with the building of the Valley Road from Hartford to Saybrook in the early 'Seventies. These in turn were followed by the Italian invasion of the end of the century. All contributed to the supply of farm labour. The Irish, however, though most of them came from the land, did not as a class turn to the land. They tended rather to herd together in the big towns and to follow in the country the work of the railways which they had helped to build. The track men were Irish. Their foreman was a man of weight in the Irish colony. He educated his boys and girls. The former very likely became firemen or brakemen and so rose to be engineers and conductors on the railway. Their ambitions included a house and garden when they settled down; and the ambition was often realised. But among the farms that I knew two only were owned by Irishmen, and these were as small as they were remote, though one of the owners was a leader in his clan and, Irish-like, something of a power in local politics. At this time most of the Irish were poor, and many very poor. Yet the men in railway employ had the advantage of steady work and pay in cash. The Irish credit was good — among the sober and reasonably frugal it was very good in my Father's estimation; so that many of these families made rapid economic and social progress. Beside the few who served the farmers, another group took care of gardens and grounds, while several became coachmen and factotums of families that needed and could afford such service, though these were not many in our quiet neighbourhood. But on the whole neither the Irish farmer nor the Irish farm labourer seemed proportionate to the men of Irish birth.

Yet in another way the Irish contributed in somewhat marked degree to the supply of competent workmen. The girls employed in domestic service were very generally Irish. Their wages were small but the frugal found saving possible. Though their schooling was meagre some of these girls had sense, competence, and physical charm enough to attract young men of the labouring class; so that as time passed a good many of them married into families of old New England blood and bore children who by right of numbers and sometimes by equal right of ability and character became an influential element in the community. Some of these grew into farm workers while not a few rose to be employers in their turn, though this was likely to be elsewhere than on the farms. A modest instance of such a union may be worth citing.

There was among the workmen of my Grandfather and Father one man of whom I was particularly fond. He had been fisherman, sailor in the coasting trade, general handy man, and farm worker, rather slow in accomplishment but entirely dependable. He was, moreover, of old Connecticut stock and bore a highly respected name; oddly enough it is fairly well established that one branch of this family through the Seymours went legitimately back to Edward III himself. This particular man and his wife were poor and when their three sons were boys poverty sometimes was rather keenly felt. All the family were at one time or another in the employ of mine. Though their wages were never large they were as much as the employment could afford. With one exception the men though of respectable habits were not of saving disposition. That exception was the second son. From his older boyhood up to middle age his monthly wage could rarely have exceeded $35; and not infrequently he must have contributed substantially to the support of his parents. But with the encouragement of his employers he saved. The savings were banked and grew. Years passed and by the time he was thirty he began to think of a home, bought a small lot from a man of substance in whose family a most respectable Irish woman had long been employed, built his house, moved his parents into it, married the girl whose savings probably helped to make the home, and reared his family, gradually adding to both house and land as the family grew.

About this time I left home for a considerable stay in the far West. A part of it was spent on the most distant plains of Texas; a part amid the mountains of Colorado. Cities and men I saw with many regions where there were neither, and all with open and interested eyes; but nothing impressed me more on my return than the house of this humble man with its surroundings. He was one of the last persons to try to make an impressive show. The house itself was plain. But it was comely; it was well-painted in the New England tradition; it had green shutters open against white clapboards; there was planting about it; its little yard was neatly mown; the street in front was clean; there was a decent shed for tools and wood; and the whole thing spoke so plainly of industry, forethought, and thrift combined with a sense of homely beauty that I thought it then and think it still to have been a memorable sight. I had seen many houses of the rich; some of their storehouses too. But these are often less impressive to clairvoyant eyes than the homes of the poor. These too generally had been ugly or neglected and barren of anything homelike and welcoming. Here were just these qualities, and it warmed my heart to find them in my native town and developed by those whose industry, self-control, patience, and purposefulness I had from boyhood watched with admiration.

Of late years the tendency has been to treat this sort of foresight and determination a little cavalierly. 'Thrift' has been at discount; and I admit that it may harden into sordidness. It has been thought to exhibit the 'profit-motive' which in turn has been assigned to the clear inspiration of the Devil. I freely grant that the profit-motive unless controlled by other and higher motives may lead to consequences of a diabolic sort. But none the less we have not passed the time when a man's desire to provide for his own by honest work, thrift, and foresight still makes for manhood; and if a day ever come, as come it may, when men and women shall look primarily to the public for such organisation of their family life and provision for their children's needs as shall relieve them from the exercise of these qualities, it is hard to believe that it will not be at the expense of slackened fibre and softened character. The rôle of 'rugged individualism' has been greatly overplayed for partisan ends; but despite this fact something remains in it without which our corporate as well as individual life must be the poorer.

It remains to ask what wages these men received. I have mentioned a wage of $35 a month as probably the maximum that the man just referred to was ever paid. He had been hired for the hay-and-harvest period of one year at $1.50 per day; but this excluded Sundays of course and rainy or very dull weather generally; so that it seems doubtful if his monthly return could have exceeded the figure mentioned. There will be those who will exclaim over the hardship to such a man of losing the dull and stormy days. They fail to grasp the situation. In point of fact a genuinely thrifty man often welcomed an interruption of this sort because it enabled him to attend to his own garden or potato field; and in this man's particular case I find records of occasional absence when he could be spared together with the use of one of the farm teams that he might do some work of his own. No estimate of the lot of such a workman can be made unless the return of his garden and field be taken into account; and one of the incidental curses of urban industrialisation is that the artisan's or mill-worker's specialised toil and huddled life deprived him not only of the opportunity but of the skill and the taste for such incidental employment.

The men who 'knew how' and who were also men of character gained much from their apparently idle time. The sea yielded clams and oysters. The winter that froze the tide-streams made eeling through the ice a laborious but to some men a profitable occupation. If the price were good eels could be sold; if poor they could be eaten. In summer berry-picking brought in something to the women and children; in husking-time there was often opportunity to husk on shares if not for wages, about one bushel in eight going to the husker; and the returns helped fill egg-basket and pork-barrel.

Generally speaking, from 1860 to the end of the century the wages of a man with a family who was hired by the year would have been about thirty dollars a month. In the bargaining process preceding agreement, an arrangement would very likely have been made for a few loads of wood or some equivalent accommodation. He would have a house and garden and the latter would very likely be ploughed for him; but they would not be rent-free, though the monthly payment would not exceed three or four dollars. There were some perquisites which seem meagre when set down in black and white, but in the aggregate were none the less of substantial account. Skimmed milk from the dairy and in their season fish and excellent fish too, from the boats were often to be had if a child were sent for them; while when beef or pork were butchered various sustaining even though secondary portions were given away. Nor were these always lacking in delicacy according to present standards. I never saw the liver of cow, calf, or pig served on my Grandfather's or Father's table; nor was the roe of a shad regarded as quite fit for any but a dubiously trained palate. These could either have been had by the first applicant for them or might be cared for and distributed to retainers who were known to need them.

In the case of boys or men who were boarded by an employer the wage might run from $15 for an older boy nearly equal to man's work to $20 for a man of strength and skill. Young boys were sometimes taken for little beyond their board and clothing, but not by our family except in one instance, when an excellent Swedish boy came with his mother who was for some time a household servant. Though rather undersized and not very strong he proved by his intelligence and industry a useful member of our staff, and though of course he went to school during term time I am confident that he was paid wages though their amount was either never known to me or has been forgotten. In any case his memories of his life with us seemed not unpleasant if his repeated letters to the family after his mother's second marriage and removal to the West meant anything.

The hours of labour were long during the period of active operations on the land; but there was never any 'sunrise to sunset' about them in the summer days. Work began at seven and ended at six with the intermission of an hour at mid-day. 'Chores' of course had to be done before and after these hours but they consisted only in milking three cows and feeding the neat stock; and for this two men were often available. Horses and fowls were cared for by members of the family. In winter the day was of necessity much shortened and in December and January could not exceed eight hours of field work. When dairying came in as a chief occupation the task of milking in the early morning added to the customary day's work was heavier than ought to have been asked except for unusual wages, though there was some slight compensation at the other end of the day when milking became part of the day's regular work instead of an added 'chore.'

By present standards the wages paid were of course inadequate. Yet they were all that the condition of farming warranted or permitted. There was no 'exploitation,' if that east-windy word has any definite meaning; at least in the declining state in which New England farming found itself no one that I knew was making any discernible gain out of the labour this rather inadequately paid. The workmen if they were temperate made at least a living; and even the intemperate very rarely came upon the town. Indeed, at this time the 'pauper' class was almost non-existent except for a few mental incompetents, invalids, and here and there some aged person who had no responsible family. There were, however, far too many who though they made a living were too meagrely supplied to develop a life fitted to improve opportunity or grapple with adversity; and in these respects I believe there has been a general improvement. Schools are better; there is more rather than less public spirit, or at least what there is seems to be more generally diffused; transportation is so much easier that it often overshoots the mark and threatens to become an end in itself. Intemperance, though still far too common, is taken somewhat less as a matter of course than it once was. The suburbanisation of the whole New England coast, though deeply regretted by many of us who knew and loved the old village life, has partially compensated for the decline of farming by offering better wages and perhaps less drudging work to dependable labourers in the care of estates and to some farmers by the purchase of land that was rapidly becoming a liability rather than an asset.

I cannot close this chapter without a word concerning the talk of these workmen among themselves. It was of course too varied and too marked by individual characteristics to be justly summarised. It was almost always interesting to me though I may have heard it in its perfectly natural state only in my very small-boyhood. Profanity was not encouraged by example on any farm I knew; nor do I remember anyone in the employ of my Father or Grandfather who was habitually and grossly profane as were some men whom I knew elsewhere, though the occasional oath was common enough. So with what might be called decency of speech; language was often coarse, jokes were broad and somewhat Rabelaisian, sexual references smacked of the barnyard; but my memories bring back little that was studiously indecent or purposefully foul, and memory may be pretty well trusted here because notorious indecency has a way of sticking in a boy's mind whether he welcome it or not. There was one man whom I greatly esteemed who had a little store of apothegms or proverbs that were both shrewd and humorous which I can no more forget than I could bring myself to repeat them in polite society (if indeed there be any such thing nowadays); but there was all the difference in the world between this man and a Canadian guide whom I once met and was unwilling to employ even for a day although he was a clever and competent man because of the quality of his talk with his fellows. In his case, strangely enough, I learned years later that his father, a most respectable and decent person to all appearance, had committed murder under strong sexual excitement and been hanged for it.

Nor were our men quite devoid of interest in what an elder time called 'philosophical themes,' though they were not matter for everyday discussion. The problems of illness and its cure came home to them of necessity; and one of the most significant things I ever heard said by one of them was the remark of an uneducated man at a time when 'fever and ague' was prevalent, to the effect that if mosquito screens were put in the windows people would not have malaria. This was while Sir Ronald Ross was still a boy and no suspicion against germ-bearing *Anopheles* had crossed the scientific mind. The man's reasoning was doubtless wrong. He probably based his conclusion upon the sight of the morning damp condensed in pearly drops upon the cotton net then used in screens. But none the less his words lingered and still seem prophetic. At the other extreme might be quoted the words of a farm workman to my Father who when a very young man had one morning announced the death of Daniel Webster. A workman spoke up and asked if he were a contractor on the Shore Line Railway which in 1852 was being built within distant sight of our homestead; yet the man was of New England birth and of an old native family.

The men who fathered the shrewd and haunting sayings of Biglow Papers type often belonged neither to the class of farmer of whom I have been speaking nor to the labourers. Both these were shrewd and clever enough in many instances but the former rarely joined the group around the stove in the village 'store' on winter evenings and the latter when he came rarely took a leading part in the conversation. There was an intermediate class, sometimes merely waggish, sometimes really wise, the best of whose chance remarks once heard cling to the memory. Such was the irony of the old man who when a neighbour whom we will call Tom Stokes was about to receive a pension was greeted with the incredulous question, 'What in the world did Tom Stokes ever do to deserve a pension?' 'Why,' was the answer as the ancient stroked a weedy beard, 'don't you know about Tom Stokes? He got overhet durin' a retreat.' Another of the same type went for a few days to New York. The line of distinction between cockney and rustic was then far more clearly marked than it is now and he was the foreordained prey of a confidence man. Before he had been long in town the inevitable stranger accosted him with great cordiality.

'How were the folks at home?' — 'How well his visit in the village was remembered.' — 'It was long ago, but not forgotten, etc., etc.' The victim swallowed it all in silence. Then came the inevitable regret: 'It's too bad, but for the moment I can't recall your name.' 'Waal,' was the quiet answer, 'I'm goin' to be daown here two or three days; p'raps it'll come to ye.'

To sum up: The life of the hired man was not ideal. It never had been. Hours were long; work was hard; wages were small. But on the other hand it was far from intolerable. The self-respecting workman was a recognised and respected member of the neighbourhood. His was the independence of a free citizen as really as that of his employer. If he were a skilled farm labourer he took satisfaction in his skill, found a modest distinction in it, and there was much variety in his work. If his wages were small, the scale of living about him was a simple one. If fire robbed him of his home or sudden illness befell, neighbours proved themselves to be neighbours indeed. The journal so often quoted shows how quick was the response of the community to the summons of calamity. This is not said to minimise the reality or even the occasional prevalence of suffering but rather to suggest the conditions that made it bearable and often robbed it of its worst bitterness. Relations between employer and employed seemed to me to be generally good. The employer worked beside his man. He was not dictatorial. The better farmers did not wish to be; if the worse tried it they found help hard to obtain. Sometimes, I know, often, I hope, relations of trust and friendship grew with the years. Some of their memories survive. If they are touched with sadness it is because they survive not only the folk but the era that gave them birth.

VIII

Field and Forest

FEW people welcome pity; and it is safe to say that most resent it. If all the facts were known, then, some of us who are country-bred must be the cause of sad resentment, since our pity has been both wide and deep for the lot of such as find their lives cramped by brick and mortar, and their eyes so dazzled by electricity that they never see the stars. Let me be frank about it. The pity has often been provincial enough — a sort of self-assertion against the seemingly greater sophistication of the town; and here and there in shallow folk not unmixed with envy. But in the true countryman the pity was real. He noted the exceeding greenness of his visitor from town. So many records of the passing seasons, open books to him, were sealed against his guest, who, greatest pity of all, showed little sense of his limitations and no desire to break the seals.

Today much of this has changed. The distinction between country boy and town boy is fading out. They wear similar clothes; see the same films; hear and speak the current slang; and each knows far more of the other's *milieu* than once could be the case. The countryman's car takes him easily and may take him often to a considerable town that reflects the life of Boston, New York, or Chicago; while the townsman manages each year his holiday in the country. So the two draw together, understand each other more quickly, benefit in some ways, and in others gravitate to a plane of mere sameness.

One would search far today to find the counterpart of a man who used to amuse my university days. He was a country boy who had made his way to town. His family was an inconspicuous one in a modest village. He had found employment in a draper's establishment; had risen, no doubt deservedly, to some small head-clerkship or perhaps to be a 'floor-walker'; and now trod city streets the image of a fashion-plate 'gentleman.' His picture is still vivid across the years: the carefully cut clothes, the blond hair and mustache as carefully trimmed, the shining silk hat, the delicate kid gloves donned even for his short walk to the restaurant where he deigned to lunch and where I sometimes saw him. We had no acquaintance; but once, when a tragic fate had overtaken a youth whom I knew, he spoke to me about the matter, and I remember his condescending reference to the victim of tragedy as a country boy who proved unable to cope with city life. Comedy and tragedy still jostle each other as I seem to hear this man-of-the-world's comment upon rusticity's invitation to disaster; and I have often pictured occasional Sundays in his native village where the silk hat, the shining boots, the lavender gloves, the mannered bearing must have had their effect; yet what would be open laughter now, then kept itself, no doubt, to an ironic smile.

The time has also passed when the average countryman in town, conspicuous by his rusticity, falls natural prey to the sharper. The villager today may seem as much at home on city streets as is the born citizen; though

his natural sense of semi-hostility to city life may well
have been actually deepened as he remembers how the
town's traffic has assaulted the village quiet that he loves
and the independence of his life been threatened by suburbanisation.

I should be the first to grant that there are some city
dwellers better fitted by nature if not by experience than
the average villager to enjoy country life; as there is
many a villager to whom the country remains but an
unwilling home and who looks forward to the time when
a happier fate shall direct his feet to pavements and his
eyes to city sights and crowds. His existence accounts in
part for the hypertrophy of our great towns. Cobbett
used to refer to London as 'The Wen'; and I have known
at least one countryman of considerable experience at
home and abroad who so habitually applied the name to
New York that his family would have remonstrated had
they not feared that if he gave up 'Wen,' implying mere
excrescence, he would shift to a worse term reserved for
a western metropolis which suggested that the tissue of
the excrescence was breaking down. It is, however, useless to bandy epithets. The dyed-in-the-wool countryman
is right about the abnormal size of our great towns. The
city dweller himself has cause to feel it as on a holiday
he tries to shake their dust from his feet when others,
bent upon the same endeavour, so throng bridge and highway with their cars or trains with their bodies that the
dust and sweat seem worse than ever.

Not thus is the country to be known. It must be one's
home; and the dweller must have the too rare but always
blessed gift of an understanding heart. The reason of
this is that the true countryman feels an inner as well as
outer relation between his life and the frame of field and

wood, hill and valley, shore and sea. Such a thing is scarcely to be accomplished by casual contact. But when a man looks upon a field and says to himself as a young man once said to me, 'I planted that crop with my own hands and in a mood of profound depression,' then he has ploughed so much of himself into its furrows that the field is his in a sort of body-and-soul relation, whoever may hold its title deeds.

Such a man knows his fields by name; and the name comes as naturally to his lips as that of one of his children. Indeed as a stranger hears the familiarity of its utterance he is half inclined to smile that a few roods of earth should be so taken up into the family circle. But to the family itself the name brings face, features, and history vividly to mind. There, for instance, is The Hill. It is 'Beacon Hill' to the world at large because for a century the United States has periodically reared landmarks on its crest for the triangulation of its Coast and Geodetic Surveys; since, though a mile inland, it commands the Sound from the Race on the east almost to Faulkner's Island on the west. But still to the family for a hundred years it has been just 'The Hill' *par excellence*, or possibly 'The Big Hill' not so much because its modest hundred feet are actually exaggerated as because they rise so abruptly from the coastal plain, limit so definitely the view to northward, and offer by their steep ascent so quick a challenge to feet used to the levels of the shore.

At its foot nestles the 'Parmelee Lot' named from a forgotten family who must once have owned it and who, if such things were remembered, might have some claim upon posterity because of its close kinship with 'The Old Oaken Bucket' and its author. Its five or six acres within their stone walls seem commonplace enough to the chance onlooker. So, no doubt, they are. But one mystery of the commonplace is that it so often lifts itself out of its own category by contact with memory. The remembered incident may be so comic, so tragic, or such an aggregate of everyday events as to constitute a major memory. When Sir Henry Taylor's Philip van Arteveldt (who now remembers him?) exclaims

> 'There is a gate in Ghent; I've passed beside it,
> A threshold there worn of my frequent feet
> Which I shall pass no more,'

he is illustrating my point. And when I think of the two gaps in this field's southern wall where two footpaths of immemorial age and use cross it, each with its worn threshold stones, his lines come back to me. This however is but a literary memory. More in keeping with the genius of the field is that of the sad forenoon when a mowing machine clipped the head from a quail sitting on her white eggs; or of the early September morning when crossing that wall I flushed a teal or two from the pond-hole where the cattle drank and later shot one (yes, and missed another) in a like pond-hole in a neighbour's field. Of course a boy's First Teal is not a minor memory. The triumph of that morning was meat and drink to me for many days. If the man who counts consistency among the major virtues should ask in his peddling way why I sorrowed for the quail and rejoiced in the Teal, I should not, perhaps could not, answer him. But I should know he never shot a teal in boyhood.

A year or two later on a day of mighty storm, one of those days when late March gathers all its energies of wind and snow to oppose the advance of Spring and, one might add, to challenge the energy and courage of a youthful gunner, I was out and cautiously approaching the western gap in this same wall. Perhaps stress of weather had driven a pair of black duck into the water-hole. No, they were not there; the afternoon was getting on; I had spent hours that morning around the sea and among the marshes in the storm; and I turned homeward not suspecting that at the other gap in the wall scarce a pistol-shot from me there lay in the deepening snow the body of an old man who had slipped and fallen in trying to cross the big stone threshold. It is possible that he reached it after my departure, but I have always thought that he was there when I came so near yet did not see him in the blinding storm. It was Monday afternoon. He was found on Thursday with only that five-or six-acre field between him and his brother's house.

Long years after when I had gone from home and made one of my own after being much up and down the earth, I went back one October day to find my Father's men husking in that same field; and was moved to sit down and work with them. Like my March snowstorm, the weather was of a rugged and memorable beauty. A great west-southwest gale was blowing out of a sky whose lanes of clear blue, through which the sun shone at times with brilliance, divided great masses of black wind-cloud. Yet it was the sort of tempest in which it was very good for a vigorous man to be alive; so vivid were the contrasts of light and shade; so trumpet-toned and confident was the announcement of approaching winter, though winter knew that its actual arrival must wait the passage of quiet Indian Summer days and misty November evenings; while we meantime were sitting close to earth, the rustling cornstalks about us, searching out, stripping, and harvesting the golden ears. There was some quiet talk and a pleasant sense of companionship in labour; but essentially we seemed almost as much creatures of the fruitful ground in our provident nearness to it that wild afternoon as were the squirrels filling their cheek-pouches under the oaks behind the near-by 'Hill' and adding the rapidly falling acorns to their winter stores. So such a field undistinguished in size or natural feature, too far out-lying also to form part of the home lands with their thronging associations, manages to establish memories and to link itself with life.

There were others with more claim to general notice. One held a long hay-barn which as it stood not far from the sea became a landmark by which I determined my position on Middle Reef; as will be told later. So inter-related in the countryman's life are such things as dis-tant barns, summer hotels, the boulders of prehistoric glacial moraines, and the dinner that he proposes to gather from the sea.

Not far from the barn was a 'swale' or slight ravine where in July or October — or both — the woodcock used to settle in their flights, and just to the north of this rose a pointed rock beside which more than a hundred years ago stood the wigwam of 'Moll Squaw,' one of the last Indians of the neighbourhood to maintain a sort of squatter's right in a cultivated field. Tradition tells of her visit to the family home to be shown my Grandmother's first baby, and her characteristically uncomplimentary remarks about the lack of beauty in the newborn of man, beast, and bird. *Gemüthlichkeit* was not the poor soul's strong point. Yet despite her failure to admire him my eldest uncle grew into a man of pleasant aspect and courteous address, a successful Boston merchant, and a master hand at catching fish and fowl. Two of his long-outmoded guns, brought from England before we made guns of first quality ourselves, still stand against my library walls and help to bring back high days on field and sea — some of them his, some mine, some ours; for he took me when I was too young, and I took him when he was too old to go alone.

Here and there a field held some unique memento of other ways and days like the lonely grave in a corner of 'The Hill.' Its brown stone with a cherub's head incised upon it told how Sybil Crane had died of small pox in 1793 and been buried there. Scarce anything could speak more clearly of the fear of a pestilence now so completely curbed as hardly to be numbered among life's perils than this burial of a young woman in a pasture remote from any group of homes and doubtless by the hands of men who had passed safely through her fatal ordeal, lest any service or burial in the public churchyard should start an epidemic. In later days a district schoolhouse stood near the corner of this pasture, and successive generations of children played over and around the grave. Perhaps Sybil Crane would have liked it to be so. The school is gone, merged in the central Public School by the march of improvement; and I fear the stone has been broken by rude and careless hands or possibly by too familiar cattle. So only a memory remains, and for its sake Sybil Crane finds place upon this page.

In Memory of
Miss Sibel Crane
Daughter of Mr. Eli
and Mrs. Mehitabel Crane
Who died with the
Small Pox May 11th
1793 in the 19th
Year of her age

Here let us turn from death to life and glance at one of the best, most companionable and rewarding of all the products of the kindly earth.

> I like flowering plants [says Alexander Smith in his unforgotten and unforgettable 'Dreamthorp']; but I like trees more, for the reason, I suppose, that they are slower in coming to maturity; are longer-lived; that you can become better acquainted with them; and that in the course of years memories and associations hang as thickly on their boughs as do leaves in summer or fruits in autumn.

I owe this particular quotation from 'Dreamthorp' to Mr. C. F. Saunders, who uses it to introduce the chapter on 'Cedars and Cypresses' in his rewarding 'Trees and Shrubs of California Gardens'; and it may very well introduce us to the groves and forests of Connecticut. Oddly enough, the Connecticut man who reads the title may find 'Cedar' familiar and 'Cypress' a little strange. Whereas in reality Cypress is familiar and Cedar really strange. He knows the 'red cedar' of the pastures; he may have cut it to support the pole-beans of his garden; he may have used it for fence or rustic arbour; he may have seen some stick of it that was driven into a salt marsh fifty years ago and pulled up yesterday sound as the day it sank as to the part below the sod. Indeed one of these little-esteemed trees may have fed his soul, as one fed mine. I used to see it rising from a minute hammock in the marshes and scarce more than a gunshot from the shore. It could have little grace for the southwest winds, sometimes bringing the salt spindrift on their wings, searched its every frond and inclined its whole top to leeward, while the great winter tides almost reached its roots. If an inquiring stranger when winter was over had asked what it did there in its loneliness and amid hard conditions,

the tree might well have answered as did the Abbé Sieyès
when asked what part he played in the French Revolution,
'*J'ai vecu.*' That was all it did. It just lived. It could not
propagate its kind. It could not attain much size. It
could not put on beauty. Yet seen in November dusks or
amid swirling snow when it was hard to hold a straight
course across the marshes, or when a high winter tide had
frozen and the expanse of ice not only hid but seemed to
deny all evidence of life, or in March wind and sunshine
as the red-salt grasses began to show golden browns
again, that tree was wondrous welcome. One might have
quoted Miss Millay and made it wave its 'banner on a
stricken hill' had the hammock been a bit higher. It was
a very steadfast little tree, and when it fell there must have
been hearts as well as eyes that missed it. *And yet it was
not a cedar, after all.*

Or if the boy who flushed the teal from the 'Parmelee
Lot' had looked northeastward that September morning
he might have seen within a quarter-mile a grove of dark-
foliaged evergreens which he and all his neighbours called
'white cedars' as distinguished from the 'red cedar' that I
have just celebrated. This 'white cedar' is, when free
from windtwists, a beautiful wood, light in weight, strong
in texture, easy to work, and with decent care very endur-
ing. Thus it has become a wood of high adventure since it
is ideal for boat-building, and so has gone not only into
every creek and harbour of the coast but into every sea as
well. Boats built of it have chased the sperm whale in the
South Seas and the bowhead in the Arctic. They have
searched the coves of stormy Desolation Island for sea-
elephants; one of them doubtless carried young Captain
Nat Palmer from his little forty-ton 'Hero' after his discovery of the Palmer Archipelago in the Antarctic to the

flagship of the Russian Admiral Bellingshausen to tell
about it; a fleet of them transported the crews of sorry
and angry whalemen from their doomed ships to the
'Sarah Adams,' when the 'Shenandoah' burned the whal-
ing fleet in Behring Sea, that Captain Hawes might see
them safe to the Sandwich Islands; and all who used their
lightness, strength, and seaworthiness had cause to bless
the 'white cedar' of New England swamps. Yet the sober
fact remains that like its red neighbour of the hills and
pastures the tree has no claim whatever to the name of
cedar except that which mistaken popular usage can con-
fer.

When I first became familiar with the hills and valleys
of New Hampshire and Vermont it was to discover that
here too there was a 'white cedar.' It was not, however,
the tree from which my fishing boats were built, but
evidently the same as the big ornamental arbor vitae
that stood in front of my home; and this I had never
thought to be a cedar. Nor is it.

Such mistakes in popular nomenclature are unfortunate.
They are not easily corrected. It seems pedantic to attempt correction, nor do I for one expect it to succeed.
Yet the honest lover of trees will face the facts. These
facts are that there is no true cedar native to Connecticut
or to any part of the United States. Cedars exist here; but
only as they have been introduced; and in Connecticut
they have been brought in so little as to make it safe to
say that but a few of those who live in Connecticut villages
have ever seen a cedar. There are at most but four varieties; some say but three; and a few astringent souls
would cut down even these to two. There is the great
'deodar' of India first known to most of us by means of
Mr. Kipling's prose and verse and to some through its

abundant growth in California; and there is the Biblical 'Cedar of Lebanon,' not now very plentiful in its native mountains, thanks to the wasteful Turk, but long ago introduced as an ornamental tree into both England and America. Some of the best I know are in the grounds of Prospect, the President's House in Princeton, and I shall always remember the pride the late Mrs. Wilson took in showing them to me on my occasional visits there when her distinguished husband was head of the University. One other variety may, I think, fairly be distinguished in the Atlas Cedar, native to the hills of Northern Africa. There is an interesting specimen in Claremont, California, and one or two very beautiful ones on the Huntington Estate near Pasadena. The doubtful fourth variety is to be found on the island of Cyprus.

Heaven forbid that anyone should think this written in derogation of our own so-called 'cedars.' Beautiful they are; useful too; and wholesome to sight and smell. But the 'red-cedar' is a juniper (*Juniperus virginiana*); the 'white cedar' of boat-building fame is a sort of cypress (*Chamoecyparis thyoides*); the 'white cedar' of New Hampshire and Vermont is, as has been said, the arbor vitae of the Thuya family. All are worthy trees, and I mourn the passing of too many of them. For though the Juniper will maintain itself in its smaller forms on our Connecticut hills and pastures, many of its larger and finer sisters in Virginia are threatened by the apple growers who fear it as a host of the apple rust. On the other hand the better it is known the more it is likely to be used as an ornamental tree. The boat-builder's 'white cedar' has become almost extinct in Connecticut. I could not now point out a single grove; nor is its ornamental value likely to save it since its love of swampy ground stands in the way of use upon the lawn; though I think it could be made to grow there and heartily wish that tree lovers would make the experiment, and that owners of estates would try it in reforesting low waste land. It will be always in demand.

The greater evergreens which once were so much in evidence have largely disappeared. The white pine was almost a rarity in my boyhood and small groups of large hemlocks like those in the Arboretum of Connecticut College in New London are fortunate indeed to find such harbourage. Yet the pine was once abundant and it is good to see it coming back on the watersheds of so many city reservoirs and in private estates. There is a tradition that the twenty-three-foot fluted pillars which upheld the entablature of the Old Lyme Church built between 1815 and 1817 were single pine trunks brought down the Connecticut, bored through the heart with a shipbuilder's pump-auger to keep them from 'checking' as they seasoned, and set up to stand in a beauty that artists loved to paint until they went up in fire in 1907. Although there is nothing impossible or even inherently improbable in this tradition, I was always a little incredulous until my presence at the burning of the Church pretty nearly convinced me. I say 'pretty nearly' because the saving of threatened homes was too urgent a business just then to leave much opportunity for antiquarian research; but the appearance of the pillars as they burned strongly suggested solid trunks. When reconstruction came the Building Committee found that replacement in a like style could only be effected by bringing firs from the far Northwest at a price that was prohibitive. If a census of mature white pines in the two towns of Old Saybrook and Old Lyme were to be taken today, I suspect that the number could be reckoned on two hands. Let us hope that despite the pine blister rust our grandsons may see better things.

Then there are trees that have individual place in successive generations because of the part they have played in public or private history. The famous Charter Oak of Hartford would be beside the purpose of this chapter were it not for my memory of certain wooden nutmegs that some ingenious person with a faint sense of humour carved from portions of it. My Grandfather had one and I think it to have been authentic. It pleased me not so much by its crude attempt at humour as by its appeal to a personal distaste; for I could wish that Connecticut might live up to its name and provide all cooks with 'nutmegs' of decent white oak; so preferable would be the tastelessness of their clean sawdust to the nauseous insipidity of the pestilent spice. There is the great elm of Wethersfield; the mighty white oak in the estate of my friend the late Doctor C. B. Graves of Gales Ferry, with its horizontal spread of more than a hundred and twenty feet — a perfect chapel for the marriage of the daughter of the family; and there is one other which must find mention here. It too is a white oak, but of that variety which loves the hammocks in the salt meadows or the fields sloping toward them. Few of these trees attain exceptional size or take on great arboreal beauty. But they are rugged, sturdy, and long-lived.

I mention this particular tree because I can trace it through so many years and because so many must have seen it across the fields to the southward and about a half-mile west of the Old Saybrook town signpost. My Grandfather was born in the year of the French Revolution and lived to so great an age that my small boyhood had the privilege of sharing his memories. He told me that he could remember that lone oak as long as he could remember any tree, and that since his boyhood he thought it had not only made no progress but that if any change had taken place it had been one of recession. This would mean that it had passed its maturity by the year 1800; and since this particular variety is of very slow growth, it would mean further that among living things the tree is one of the oldest monuments of our shore towns. It may well endure for a century or two longer since on my last visit its vitality still seemed strong; and when it falls — Heaven forbid that it should ever be cut — I hope some friendly eye and pen will note and record its age. At present it is in wise and loving hands. May they be strong to hold it!

Here time and space fail me as they failed the writer of the Epistle when he spoke of memorable lives. For I would fain speak of forest paths and the sights they brought me; of the vanished chestnuts, slowly but surely coming back I trust, and of the autumn harvests gathered under them, sometimes with my Father who had the habit of counting the nuts as he picked them up so that when pockets bulged and sagged he could still tell how many he had. Of hickories too, generally of the *glabra* variety and therefore with hard-shelled nuts — we had few shagbarks — but worth gathering partly for their own sakes and partly because they came so late that the time for other plunder had passed. There was one open park-like field that had a mighty chestnut in its midst and others along its southern wall while hickories gave variety to its eastern border which was a great favourite with us. As one passed through it and approached an eighty-acre woodlot of our own the trees grew denser. The tulip was here forced to assume its flagpole habit running up

branchless sixty or seventy feet; birches and soft maples
grew aplenty; there were oaks, too, white and yellow (we
never spoke of the 'red-oak' as do the books). In open
glades the mountain laurel grew and was known locally as
'ivy.' There was no great amount of beech but enough to
make it well known.

This always seemed to me one of our most beautiful
trees and I have wondered why it has not found greater
place on our lawns and along our roads. It is true that
grass is impatient of its shade but one cannot have everything and the beauty of its smooth grey trunk, the fresh-
ness of its spring leaves, the denseness and long contin-
uance of its foliage, all help to make it notable. Even
yet however what is perhaps its greatest claim to consideration awaits a mention. This is the almost unique
distinction of its winter habit with interlaced branches
and branchlets so delicate yet so sturdy and all pointed
with the long leaf-buds. In this it contrasts with the ash
which is a noble tree and gives much dignity as well as
beauty to the roads about New London; yet it disappoints
one in winter by the bluntness, not to say clumsiness, of its
crown. Both beech and ash are good trees under the axe
and in the fire. The former lends itself to the turning
lathe and makes our bowls and other kitchen utensils;
the ash supplies us with handles to forks, rakes, and
numberless other tools: while working oars (as distinguished from those of mere rowboats) are so generally
made of it that a 'white-ash breeze' has on the coast become a synonym of calm. I lift up an axe without much
compunction against an ash greatly as I respect it. But
there are three beeches in a wood where my men and I
often work that challenge me each winter. Yet I cannot
cut them. They are still growing; they are so exquisitely

smooth; so strong yet so delicate; their branches make such reticulation against the winter sky; that though my axe head instinctively turns its edge toward them, as the official axe-bearer used to turn his toward the prisoner after conviction of treason to show the onlookers that he had been found guilty, season after season I pass them by, glad of so much beauty that I hope will still be growing when I'm sleeping.

As we go along our woodland path a teamster who, we will suppose, is our companion suddenly stops before a straight, strong shoot that holds a leafy top some ten feet in the air, considers it a moment, draws his knife, and cuts it 'for a cartwhip' he says. If asked what the little staddle is he is likely to give a vague reply. It will be no confession of ignorance. He will have his name for it. But this may be 'rock elm,' or possibly 'ironwood'; and you will feel that your knowledge has not much increased. A bit further and another tree that at first you think may be a beech, and whose leaves have a certain resemblance to the birch, claims his attention. This too he examines: then reaches for the axe in its cleat somewhere about his cart-body, cuts it down, trims it out, and puts the trunk, some two inches through at the butt and perhaps ten feet long into the cart. This is to serve as a 'binder' for his load of wood, twisting the chain that goes about it. Questioned again as to the name of the little tree he is far more likely to say 'ironwood' than in the former case and he may say 'blue beech' or 'hardbeam.' The last name is pretty nearly right; for both these tough, strong, highly resilient trees are hornbeams. Every locality seems to have its 'ironwood'; but so far as I have been able to discover it generally is one form or the other of the hornbeam. The cartwhip variety is the hop-hornbeam (*Ostrya virginica*) and if the traveller up the Great Lakes will stop at Mackinac Island in early August he will find the tree growing to considerable size and laden with great drupes of fruit like hops. This explains its name; but I do not remember ever to have seen its fruit in southern Connecticut. The other hornbeam with its grey buttressed trunk, and such general likeness to the beech that 'blue beech' seems appropriate, is the *Carpinus caroliniana*.

Shrubs meanwhile cry out on every hand for notice, and richly deserve it. If the trees withdraw to make room for pasture land we shall run upon the sumac in its two or three harmless varieties, especially if the land be hilly; but if it turn swampy, then beware of a shrub which may reach the size of a little tree, a cousin of the staghorn sumac, the bearer of graceful branchlets and of drupes of wax-like berries, with foliage of such thrilling brilliance in late September as to betray many an unwary hand into gathering it. The presence and glory of this sumac, indeed, is a feature of the journey by rail from Saybrook to Boston when its leaves are turning, so frequent is it and so instant is its challenge to the eye. It is of course the *Rhus vernix* or *venenata*, the poison sumac or 'poison elder' of the shore towns and the most to be feared of the two poison plants we have. The United States Forestry Bulletins, I am sorry to say, are making a Toxicodendron family of the poison ivy, the poison elder, and the absurdly named poison oak of the Pacific Coast and calling them *Tox. radicans*, *Tox. vernix*, and *Tox. obtusa* or *diversilobum*. I am sorry, because it seems as though the accustomed *Rhus toxicodendron*, *Rhus vernix*, etc. helped by its reminder of caution when contemplating any member of the sumac clan.

From this approach to treason let us turn to a shrub as

wholesome in branch, flower, and fruit as the poison
sumac is dangerous; and its rival in autumn beauty. It
comes to its best some time after the sumac has faded and
matches the oaks in its late glory. Drive from Lyme to
New London by the shore road after you have thought the
autumn foliage has faded because your maples have 'gone
by' and see how the Vaccinium (the high bush blueberry)
will reward you. Or look for it in Spring when you are on
horseback and can ride up close enough to mark the
delicacy of colour and of form with which it gives its
promise of foliage and fruit for the coming season. Then
go your way to ponder on the insoluble problem of
whether the grace of May or the splendour of October is
the better; and if you be wise, settle it by claiming both.

In conclusion a word must be said about the companionship which work in grove and forest brings. There
is something about the quiet of the woods even on windy
days that induces quietness of mind. The work is wholesome; it is too exacting for industrious men to spend much
breath in talk. But it is co-operative work in a very
real sense. My Father made it a rule never to send a
man to work in the woods alone. It is a good though
not an inexorable rule. Accidents too easily happen,
and when they happen help is likely to be too remote.
So there is a real though unexpressed and quite unsen-
timental sense of interdependence that generally makes
for good fellowship. One is always learning something,
too. A white oak, inadequately scored on the side opposite the saw, will when falling split its trunk up and
leave its heavy butt standing on a substantial splinter of
itself eight feet in the air, a very deadfall to the careless
axe-man who tries to bring it down. Or on a frosty morning when logs are to be split the frozen wood will not admit

a wedge but spits it spitefully out; and one will learn that
for every three wedges of mild steel there should be one of
iron, since the latter bites so much better than the former
when frost is in the wood.

Then there are confidences begotten of quiet. I shall
not forget the sudden remark of a most worthy and
generally reserved man with whom I came out one afternoon our axes on our shoulders. We passed a small house
a-building. 'I hoped once' said he, 'that I should some day
have a little place like that. I never shall.' It was probably but too true. He had employment, friends, frugality;
but family illness and its demands were calling him to
another country and into circumstances that guaranteed
the soundness of his sad prophecy. A more cheerful
atmosphere surrounded my old Irish gardener and me as
one afternoon we reached a barway across the cartpath
that brought us to our work. He was of the elder type of
Irishman who had training, manners, and so much self-
respect that he liked to be respectful. We had both been
silent thinking our own thoughts when suddenly and
à propos of nothing James said: 'You know, Sir, the three
Mr. Cassidys all had a college eddication.' It was as
irrelevant as the remark 'there's milestones on the Dover
Road' with which Mr. F.'s Aunt used to enliven the
conversation in 'Little Dorrit,' and it was with a smile
that I expressed my satisfaction at the advantages enjoyed by the Messrs. Cassidy although I had never heard
of them before. Then James took me into the land of far
away and long ago where he had been dwelling and introduced me to 'Mr. James,' 'Mr. Philip,' and 'Mr.
Charles,' real people to him still though he had left Ire-
land and their home when little more than a boy. It was a
small happening and years have intervened; yet the day

with its weather, the slant of the afternoon sun, the autumn quiet, the very position of the old man with reference to myself as we walked together are etched in memory. As years pass such memories adorn field and forest in growing multitudes. They are wholesome and they touch the face of nature with a grateful humanity.

IX

The Salt Meadows

IT was years ago. December had brought hard frost; so hard indeed that a high tide flooding the marshes had frozen before it could wholly ebb, and the meadow surface was covered with corrugated ice. The weather had moderated a little and the sun was shining palely; but it was winter none the less. For a youth still feeling the inspiration of his first gun it was almost too mild and calm. Ducks could hold the sea instead of seeking the quiet and food of the tide creeks. Yet any weather was worth trying; and so the early afternoon found him with a friend, gun on shoulder, moving shoreward. A little boat — a very little boat which could be pulled out of water and overturned safe from floating ice and drifting snow — served as ferry across two creeks and into a broad expanse of salt meadow that was practically an island.

Then began a stealthy reconnaissance. Each pool in the meadow was examined. Each reach of the creek that the ebb tide had nearly emptied was looked at from some coign of vantage where a slowly raised head might escape the keen eye of a watching black duck. Shell ice was avoided and voices were controlled, for it was an open question whether the duck's eye or ear were the keener.

At last three birds were discovered feeding in a broad reach that was almost bare, and so far from the nearer bank as to rob it of much of its value as cover. There seemed little chance of successful approach by ordinary methods. So recourse was had to stratagem. There was a consultation and subsequent retreat to a roughly wooded hammock in the marsh. There search in the long undergrowth revealed a rude sled, or the framework of one. On it were two uprights with brackets to hold a gun. Across these was fastened a frame of lath with long marsh grass between the stringpieces; and this was high enough to form a cover for a gunner that was at once practicable in extent and natural in character provided it was used with discretion. The thing was put in condition after its exposure to the December weather and the advance began.

It was a long crawl. For a little way the gunner could crouch behind his blind and use his feet. Then came the slow advance on his knees over the rough ice. He must needs stop now and then to lift a cautious head behind the screen of grass with a view to observation not only of the ducks but of his own progress from the ducks' point of view; for the screen itself must inevitably be revealed to them long before he could come within decent range. This was of course expected, and the blind of wavy grass was like enough to the frost-bitten sedge that sparsely lined the creek's bank to excite no alarm unless it were moved too suddenly along the ducks' skyline. Its movement to and fro in the light wind which fortunately blew from the birds to the gunner was perhaps an advantage since such familiar swaying tended to divert attention from its gradual mass movement.

The famous pilgrim whose penance consisted of a journey with peas in his shoes might have sympathised with the slow and painful progress of the gunner on his knees over those little wavelets of ice. There was no avoiding them and they made their presence increasingly felt despite the thickness of winter clothing and the natural excitement of the chase — if chase it could be called. To be sure the pilgrim boiled his peas and got on better. Some day the sun would in like fashion soften the gunner's way, though if he crawled through water he might easily wish himself on ice again.

At last the bank drew near and the ducks were still undisturbed. The sled was now turned directly toward them so that all further advance was foreshortened and there was no lateral movement of the screen. At this point the reader, if he be a gunner, is ready to ask if we are to take a pot shot at sitting birds. We are if we can and there is nothing unsportsmanlike about it as he would well know if he had ever tried this sort of shooting. Indeed it is doubtful even yet if it can be managed so keen is the eye of the black duck to discern the slightest unnatural movement in its surroundings. This makes it difficult even to aim through the screen without alarming the fowl; and in any event the distance is so great and the shot used necessarily so heavy in order to carry it that the case is altogether different from that of the use of a puntgun perhaps fired from a swivel with its big charge of Number 4 or Number 6 shot at a flock of sleeping or resting birds. In the present instance the three duck, though fairly close together, lay across the line of aim. One's best chance was at the middle bird in hope that a stray shot might reach a neighbour on one side or the other. Slowly — ah, how slowly — the muzzle of the gun was wormed through the thin screen, aim was taken, the trigger pulled and the reasonably expected result noted. The middle bird kept his place in the creek. His fellows rose. The second barrel dropped one on the creek's further bank. The other went to sea. A brave little retriever, an old-fashioned terrier that never refused the water however full of floating ice, brought out the bird in the creek. The gunner crossed the creek's mouth which was easily fordable at low tide, and picked up the victim on the further bank, his youthful heart so thankful for the pair as to waste no regrets upon the other duck's escape.

But even here there was a sequel. The next day falling upon Sunday, the gunner as was his custom went to church; took a back seat as youth is wont to do; and found himself beside a much older man whom he knew well. This man was a scion of an old village family generally as poor in substance as it was rich in intelligence. It had given to New England its first calculator of almanacs and in a later generation one of its best-known physicians and writers upon Materia Medica. The diary of my seat-mate's grandfather is now in my possession with its occasional entries in Latin though it is doubtful if the author ever went beyond the village school. He himself was very likely the best informed resident of the community upon its local history and his family papers are still searched by town historians. Yet in a notable degree he lacked what are called 'practical gifts'; he had extremely meagre resources; and it was probably a matter of consideration for the larder that had led him on the previous afternoon to the 'clam flats' with hoe and basket. At any rate, he had been there within a half-mile of the gunning episode. And when as the service proceeded a hymn was announced and we shared a hymnbook, the elder leaned forward to whisper to the younger, 'I picked up your other duck yesterday.' There is no record of the hymn's first line or of the preacher's text; but the service abides in memory as one of extraordinary uplift.

'Why?' some reader may ask, especially if he be of the sort afflicted with an appetite for tyrannous consistency; 'why should a youth of at least rudimentary intelligence and who had enjoyed reasonably good opportunities for its cultivation; who was not of cruel temper and who had a distinct fondness for animals — why should he care to remember after many years seemingly with thanksgiving the spending of a Saturday afternoon in outwitting and killing three harmless birds?' Why, indeed? I cannot answer my critical friend to his satisfaction unless, as is very likely the case, my inability is itself satisfying because it seems to put me so clearly in the wrong. I can only say that the spirit of adventure still abides in normal youth; and that some traces of the feral instinct are not uncommon. Nor are these in themselves to be altogether lamented. The spirit of adventure not only gives zest to living but opens paths of advance along intellectual as well as material lines; while the feral instinct though quite as capable of abuse as the instinct of sex, still when restrained helps make a man into that very useful person whom the typical Yankee of my boyhood called a 'good provider.' I always liked to hear a man called that. A picture rose before me of one who did a good day's work when he found it and had moreover a gift of finding it pretty regularly; one who saw to it that its returns in money or produce were duly conserved for his family's support; and further than this one who could turn time when he was out of work to service of the household either at home or by making field, forest, and sea pay him tribute abroad. This gift for bringing something home develops early in some youngsters and if the something is honestly come by is almost always to the good.

It was part of our code that creatures harmless in themselves while living and useless to us when dead should go unscathed, and this code was pretty well observed. I think we were honest too in our purpose to shoot to kill rather than wound and not to shoot at all unless there was a chance of retrieving our game. Where the code fell short was in failing to protect some fowl that returned a very minor reward to the gunner and some rare visitors, like an occasional egret for instance, that should have been welcomed and guarded as is now the case instead of being shot as 'specimens'; though it should be said that despite my somewhat incredulous quotation marks, they often did become genuine specimens in the cabinet of a nearby naturalist, and perhaps fulfilled their destiny as well there as if they had fallen victims to old age or to some vagrom hawk.

Edible ducks like the black duck, the occasional mallard, the very delicious teal, and the broadbill were used as completely as domestic fowl, feathers, wings, and body. The grebe family was rarely disturbed — it should have gone completely free — since it was not only inedible but difficult to get without a waste of ammunition; but even here its very beautiful breast plumage did service on hat or muff, though this did not justify the sacrifice.

But the story of the marshes and their rewards is never to be told in terms of game brought home. One never got large bags. Often one brought back nothing, sometimes because there were no ducks in the meadows, sometimes because though there they could not be reached, sometimes most lamentable of all because one's shooting was bad. For this last there was no balm but forgetfulness or the pulling off of a difficult shot next time; then all was forgiven. As to the other sources of failure there were compensations, inadequate perhaps at the time but in the

aggregate returning great and memorable reward. There
was one's acquaintance with weather in all its phases,
especially its rougher ones. I have stood on Cornfield
Point on a bright and bitter winter afternoon when the
sludge ice reached in a line as far as I could see toward
Plum Island and a small boat caught in it might never
have got free. Again in such cold that the creeks were
closed and the shore barricaded with ice-floes grounded
by the ebb of recent tides, such cold that my gun barrels
coated themselves with frost at once upon entering a
warm room at home, I watched with interest the search
of a field mouse among the great ice-cakes for some trifle
that would keep the breath of life and spark of warmth
in his little body. He had small luck while I looked on
but I still hope that a sedge root or some bit of flotsam
or jetsam rewarded his endeavour. This was a day of
storm from the sailor's rather than the landsman's stand-
point for the sun was brilliant though the cold was cruel
and the northwest wind was strong. There were other
days, too, some of them still memorable, when all nature
seemed to conspire against life. Such was the March
morning of wind and driving snow when I peered over the
sandbank of a jutting point to see whether there might
not be a duck or two among the rocks. In a gap between
two of these I saw a duck's head, took what aim I could at
the small object and fired. Suddenly the air above my
little target held a half dozen birds and I was angry with
myself for failing to see more than my one duck and then
missing him. There was nothing for it but to stand up and
face my failure. But on standing I caught a glimpse of
fluttering feathers and, lo, there was my duck after all
dead as the doornail of tradition. None the less I should
have done better though but a schoolboy at the time.

But great as this storm was it pales into something approaching insignificance when compared with the Great Blizzard of 1888. That is what assured me of the unique severity of the latter. Used as I was to weather, rejoicing in it indeed, and sometimes vexing my Mother a little by a tendency to go out into the worst apparently just for the sake of it, I have never faced a storm that was quite fitted to measure the power of the Blizzard. It began in the night between Sunday and Monday; and by mid-forenoon its character as a tremendous storm had established itself. Yet the ways were not yet blocked, trains were moving, and two of my much younger brothers had gone to school in a nearby town. In spite of the fact that I had been in-valided home from the University, though not acutely ill, my own thoughts turned instinctively to the meadows. There must surely be ducks; and ducks as it proved there were, but about as safe from any harm that I could do them as though my gun had been left at home. Before the great north gale my little boat skimmed down the lower reach of one creek and across the mouth of two without any effort on my part except to keep it before the wind; and with a celerity that already set me thinking that getting back might present unusual problems.

Then came the revelation. The tide should have been half down. Instead the creeks were full, water flooded the lower meadows, and there seemed no chance or promise of its dropping. Ducks were in sight but the water was so high that almost all the usual cover was valueless. If I could have stayed — but there was the rub. The storm was growing worse. Getting back, which had been merely an academic question when first thought of, was already pressing and the next hour might make it vital. I could not even tell how long the water on the meadows would

permit me to regain my boat now secure but already floating on a bank rarely overflowed. For once ducks had to
retreat to second place. I turned boatward, but could not
look toward it except for a moment at a time, and despite
complete familiarity with the terrain found myself yielding direction a little to the tremendous wind, though fully
alive to the danger of doing so. The boat was, however,
reached at last. The passage to be made was not a long
one and usually was the simplest matter imaginable. But
today the common mouth of the two tide-creeks was a
raging sea as compared with its ordinary quiet; and for the
only time in my life I took my oilskin coat off to have
freer scope in case of a capsize. Ice or half-melted snow
tended to gather on my oars though the cold was not yet
extreme. I knew that the main thing to do was to hold my
little boat's head to the sea and take my time about
getting across; better slow progress than a capsize. Once
and only once an icy oar slipped up on a thole-pin and the
bow fell off; but it was quickly caught and brought to the
wind again, and slowly, very slowly we gained the wished-
for bank. The size of the boat had constituted a danger
but it may also have been a condition of safety for had it
been larger I doubt if it could have been forced to windward. It was hauled out, turned over, left to the storm,
and I gratefully fought my way home.

And still the storm grew until at night when I ventured
out to a neighbour's to discover if any news had come
from the boys in their distant school I thought the wind
would suck the breath from my lungs when my back was
turned and gag me with its force when trying to face it.
The distance was perhaps sixty rods before the wind on
the way over, and into it of course on the return, and I
doubt if the return could have been achieved had not a

stable or shed given me rest and shelter when half-way and a slat fence enabled me to climb to its second rail and so move sidewise a foot at a time above the deepest of the snow; for it was almost impossible to force a way through it when the wind demanded all one's energy.

Weather was a part of our business, and the acceptance of its challenge our frequent pleasure in those youthful shooting days; but that March outbreak of northern fury remains, I think, unique in the experience of everyone who faced it; and the toll of those who were too old to endure the exposure and exertion thrust upon them and who later died of their effects must have been large in town and country alike. One man, later well known to me, lame but otherwise of rugged physique, finding himself overtaken and perhaps confused in the fields had the good sense to seek the shelter of a wall, let the snow cover him, and to find himself next day little the worse for his adventure. A Boston–New York express foundered in the drifts within a half-mile of my home, stayed there over night, a little later managed a retreat to the nearest station and resumed its journey in the middle of the week. All in all it was the most memorable of storms since the historic 'September Gale' of 1815; and none who tasted its power wished to repeat the experience.

Lest the reader should suppose that rough weather was the necessary concomitant of salt meadow walks I hasten to record a day in Spring which befell many years later than those just mentioned. It was too late to expect a duck but a handful of snipe might be gleaned and I set out with the walk rather than the game uppermost in mind. Perhaps it will momentarily assuage the severity of tender-minded critics who count all killing of game a slightly mitigated murder if I add that it is doubtful if a shot were fired that morning. But the memory is clear enough of a few minutes' halt on the northern edge of a peninsula of upland that jutted into the marshes. It was wooded in a parklike way with tough and sometimes distorted white oaks. Here and there was a small pond where a black duck might sometimes be flushed though, as I have intimated, it was now too late to shoot birds that had mated and might be nesting. Once in a great while amid the bunches of bay and berry bushes an old sow might be disturbed who would rush off in a kind of fury with the odd 'Whiff, whiff,' which Sir Samuel Baker used to say characterised the African rhinoceros; and after it one walked on pondering the likeness between domestic and savage pachyderms.

On such a day I came out to the northern margin of Long Point and looked across Back Creek to the fields and distant village beyond it. Spring ploughing was in process and the good brown earth sunned itself in preparation for the seed. Here and there a team was at work. The white houses stretched along the Point and Post Roads for some two miles, every one of them known to me. An almost Sabbath quiet brooded over everything. Colour was coming back in delicate greens and golden browns into the meadow grass. A breeze just rippled the water in the creek; the ripples played with the sunbeams; and one realised how lovely a thing even a humble tide-creek can become when its muddy banks have clothed themselves with the incoming tide. It was a rare picture, and its significance was greater for memories of the two and a half centuries through which year by year men had first cleared and pastured, then ploughed, sown, and reaped these fields. Some families had kept at this good work since the old town was settled. Others had gone far afield or sailed around the world. Here to the left lay the home of one family a member of which if tradition be trustworthy had helped to settle one of the great industrial and cultural cities of central New York and then, moved by the pioneer instinct, had gone further west to 'cut the first tree on the site of Milwaukee' — a feat I do not vouch for but which is by no means impossible. Beyond a group of trees not far from the town's centre lived a commander of famous packet ships between New York and England whose list of acquaintances, many of whom became personal friends, would read like a roster of some of the most famous names in English and American letters with a generous sprinkling of leaders in political and social life. A bit to the westward was the friendly home of one who as Commissioner of Police in New York probably did more than any other man to save the city in the days of the Draft Riots of 1863 when the Irish mob was murdering negroes and threatening universal fire and pillage. Beyond these and to the north stood the house out of which came the brides of Commodore Isaac Hull of 'Constitution' fame and of his nephew, also a Commodore. Another sailor of an elder day who seldom brought his ship into the Connecticut when he came home and who was reputed to be a slaver lived just on the borders of my vision. I scarce know whether or not to put on record his probable[1] pilotage of a lawless French squadron against Sierra Leone and Zachary Macaulay in those French Revolutionary days when the latter, still a bachelor, was doing his best to bring order out of the colony's chaos. I say 'still a bachelor' because during the French invasion a pistol was put to Macaulay's breast and I have sometimes felt a

[1] The circumstantial evidence is convincing; the lack of a first name is the only break in the chain of direct evidence.

twinge of deep concern as to what might have happened to
English Literature had it gone off with fatal effect as it
might easily have done. Where then would have been
Thomas Babington with his letters to Sister Hannah?
where the History? the Essays? the Indian Code? the
Lays, so dear to schoolboys and those like-minded from
eight to eighty? where Hannah herself? and therefore
where the Trevelyans, Sir George Otto and George
Macaulay? where the 'Life and Letters of Lord Macaulay,'
the 'Early Life of Charles James Fox' and the ill-arranged
but none the less priceless 'American Revolution' which
must long stand chief among histories by Englishmen for
generous appreciation of the American side and an endeavour to be fair that sometimes leans backward?
Where too the long list of studies by the Professor of
Modern History in the University of Cambridge?

I am far from saying that all this passed through my
mind on that spring morning as I sat in the sunshine with
my gun beside me. But much of it has entered into my
experience of these salt meadows; and behind it all has
been the assurance that much of the character of the quiet
men who have stayed upon these fields and won their
living from them and much of the effectiveness of those
who went abroad, have been gained on the physical side
from experience of such vicissitude of climate as this chapter has suggested. It was no light thing to make a living
on this southern coast. But it was a practicable thing for
men of energy, endurance, and intelligence sufficient to
cope with and to bring into some sort of harmony winter
and summer, storm and sunshine, upland, marsh, and sea
with their diverse change and chance.

I cannot leave the meadows without paying tribute to
them for their service in two other particulars. One never

knew when some new form of fowl would turn up or some
odd experience be offered. For instance, on the Saturday
following the Blizzard I caught a glimpse of a bird on the
edge of the sea that at first looked like a large duck.
Looking again, as he raised his wings and arched his neck
he seemed certainly to be a goose. On securing him he
proved to be the only brant or brent-goose that I ever saw
in our marshes or coves, though they are not uncommon
on Cape Cod and in the Great South Bay region. Some
years later an even rarer visitor came my way. A sombre
November afternoon was darkening toward evening. It
was slightly misty, too, and I was just turning homeward
when a sound like the yapping of a small dog attracted my
attention as it came down the light easterly wind. Wondering at it and listening I heard something that suggested
the call of a goose, though quite unlike the well-known
'honk' of the Canada variety; stood still and crouched a
little; and presently saw a line of five or six fowl that were
unquestionably geese but such as I had not seen before.
They came by. It was a long shot and I could scarcely see
the sight of my gun. But I fired and thought I heard the
shot strike the last bird; gave him the other barrel,
brought him down, and wondered what I had. It proved
to be the only Snow Goose that I ever saw in our region.
He was taken to the neighbour-naturalist already referred
to, skinned, and the carcase hung out through a cool
November night. Whether it was the frost or the fact
that he was probably a gosling of the previous Spring I do
not know, but the flesh proved to be in perfect condition
for cooking and I never tasted a better bit of wild-fowl.
His skin excellently mounted long adorned my neighbour's
cabinet of specimen birds.

But the oddest part of this very small adventure was

yet to come. Not less than fifteen years afterward I was
talking with the late Henry Noyes of Old Lyme, a lineal
descendant of one of the founders of Yale, and a man who
had gone far afield in his youth and done a good deal of
shooting in California when that state was young. He
mentioned the snow goose as not infrequent there, and
went on to say that once he had been surprised to see a
small bunch flying over Lyme. I was interested and asked
when. It was years before, he was sure, but we finally
traced the matter back with a particularity that made me
certain that my bird had flown over Lyme and been
identified by almost the only man in the vicinity who
could have known it on the wing; then had come to Saybrook to my gun and table; and finally joined California
and Connecticut in a common experience. The Blue
Goose, which is so often found with the Snow Goose as to
lead some observers to think they interbreed, has long
been a mystery in respect of its nesting grounds; and only
within recent years have these been discovered upon the
desolate western shore of Baffin Land above Fox Channel
and not far from the bleak Spicer Islands bearing the
name of a well-known whaleman from Groton, Connecticut.

There are doubtless those who shoot over decoys cooped
up in blinds or sunken boats to whom this method of
gunning in the meadows must seem a waste of time and
energy. If size of bag be their main consideration they are
right. There are others who never shoot at all who will
not understand even when they are told why a man
should carry a gun for miles, even without firing a shot,
and be ready to repeat the experience on his next half-
holiday. This chapter is not for them. Telling would be
vain. But there are others still whose memory brings

back miles of happy walking under sun and cloud with just enough excitement to season time and make weariness rewarding. It was a healthful business. I well remember one afternoon when things looked rather drab and desolate, when long-continued strain of overwork with brief intervals of too strenuous exercise had exacted their toll of depression, when there was little chance of game but walking with a gun seemed better than nothing. Suddenly out of a most unlikely bit of a hole in the meadow, astonishing me quite as much as I had disturbed him, in a rare twitter and with great uprush of wings a big mallard drake burst into the air — a splendid bird; and when he fell to my first barrel I felt that after all a frayed and overwrought system was not in such bad case as I had feared; that old-time vigour would return again and the rainbow regain some of its lost colours.

It was, I repeat, a sound life that we lived with our guns in the marshes; wholesome in respect of physical health; in its demand for constant alertness; in the acquaintance established with manifold forms and phases of Nature; in establishing memories that may outlast life; and not least in affording opportunity for the long, long thoughts of youth.

X

The Sea

DO YOUR
  'Yesterdays look backward with a smile,
  Nor wound you like the Parthians as they fly?'
It was Eliot Warburton somewhere in the middle of last
century questioning his friend, R. M. Milnes, who later
became Lord Houghton; and the problem is one of perennial importance. I think that boys and young men whose
holidays were spent after the manner suggested in the last
chapter among the marshes and, as I now propose to indicate, upon the sea can generally be counted on for an
answer as confident as it is happy. In travelling recently
I chanced to find in the smoking room of a Pullman car a
young man of college student age who though carelessly
dressed yet bore himself like a gentleman and encouraged
casual conversation. A college student he proved to be
and my suspicion that he had a pinch of salt in his system
was correct. Having just brought his cruising boat into
the Connecticut for the winter he was on a train for the
first time in months. With engaging frankness he admitted
that college work while pleasant enough was not so congenial but that it required all his resolution to keep it
upon a respectable level. He did it, but under some feeling

of constraint. Yet I venture the surmise that when tri-
gonometry entered upon its navigational phase this young
man's work did him credit. The sea was in his blood; not
the slang and bluster of the stage- or 'movie-' sailor — not
a bit of it. On the contrary he was quiet, frank, courteous,
and of a naïve simplicity that suggested depth rather than
shallowness of experience. One felt how educative his recent life on the Maine coast and in the Bay of Fundy had
been; how much of alertness, watchfulness, and competence in weighing the change and chance of weather
had been developed; how he must have grown in knowledge of his craft's ability to stand sail, in the wisdom or
folly of testing this ability at night, and in acquaintance
with the mighty tides and the treacherous tendency of
currents great and small to falsify dead reckoning, especially in fog.

Now, these influences make for education and tend to
explain why men bred in youth to the sea so often develop
an 'all-round' competence on land. The call of the deep
sea had pretty much ceased to ring in the ears of boys on
our coast at the time of which I write. The day when the
sea captains of Old Lyme, Essex, Old Saybrook, and West-
brook had been leading citizens of their towns, carrying the
tang of blue water into the day's common business and
sometimes bringing the voice of the quarterdeck into the
sacred precincts of town meeting, had passed by. Few
boys went to sea in the older meaning of that term though
some in humble station still shipped on 'coasters,' others,
a little more ambitious, fitted themselves for the engine
rooms of tugboats or river steamers, and there were always candidates enough for any position about wharves
or dockyards. Shipbuilding was over; but boat-building
still went on.

And with boat-building begins my story of one of the best educational and, I dare to add, cultural chapters in the development of some of us. It was not the mere fabrication of boats that furnished this. That taught us something, for we used to build our own very primitive punts for crabbing in the summer and shooting in the winter, even venturing out to the reefs in some of these when the weather omens seemed trustworthy. We went further and built 'sharpies' as our flat-bottomed craft were called — quite flat-bottomed if used exclusively for rowing, but provided with skag and centreboard if meant for sailing, for which some of them were abundantly competent. I still remember the first built by another boy and myself out of such odds and ends as we could pick up about our respective homes; and wonder, recalling its composition and use, that I survive to tell of it. The next year we built another and since my companion was really a mechanic even though a very young one and we went down into our shallow pockets for the essential materials instead of depending upon mere flotsam and jetsam, this turned out to be a decent and seaworthy boat. Later on with the assistance of a neighbour, both good craftsmen though neither was a professional boatwright, he built a substantial craft in which I cruised many miles to sea and saw some rough weather.

But the type of craft that commanded both my respect and affection was modelled upon that of the gill-net fishermen of the Connecticut River. This latter was an open boat except for a little cuddy forward and a six-inch washdeck. It had a centreboard. The sail was a spritsail and the mast was set into a half circle cut in a heavy forward thwart. Here it was firmly clamped by a semi-circular collar of iron hinged at one end and slipped over a staple at the other where a pin locked it. The sail when the sprit was removed could of course be furled closely to the mast, the mast easily lowered, and the whole thing thrust to one side while the boat was under oars or tending net. Originally clinker (or clencher) built these boats were later almost always carvel-built — which signifies, I may be permitted to explain, a smooth side with strake laid edge to edge with strake, as on a caravel, instead of having the strakes overlapped or clenched. Both forms of construction were good, and I inclined to think the clinker-built a little drier in a sloppy sea. But when it grew old and tender or began to leak, caulking was difficult because it tended to force the overlapping strakes apart and 'the rent was made worse.' The carvel form with its square abutting edges lent itself very happily to caulking when that necessity arose.

These were small boats rarely exceeding eighteen feet in length and six or six and a half in width; they were as able as they were convenient; one man could row them, though he might be loth to do so; two could handle them very well under oars; while under sail they were swift and quick in stays, though the broad-headed spritsail was not the most effective sailing rig for them. It was, however, essential to the river fisherman because it could so easily be put out of the way.

Two builders in Essex, Henry Tucker and a man named Hurlburt, put out most of the sailboats I knew. Tucker's boats were perhaps a little more impressive because they had a higher freeboard that suggested power. But Hurlburt's type, though a trifle lower and seemingly more open, were on the whole as perfectly adapted to our uses as could be imagined. The tide-creeks were our harbours. Most of these lacked channels at their mouths. The rise and fall of our tides could not have averaged more than three and a half feet; and dead low water meant scarcely a foot of depth where a trace of channel debouched into the Sound among the outer sand flats. This situation called for the least possible draft consistent with safety in the outer waters. Hurlburt's design and craftsmanship met the need admirably. The particular boats I knew best, as distinguished from the generality mentioned above, were little more than sixteen feet long and of ample beam. There was a fair amount of sheer, and though the freeboard amidships may have seemed scant, the lines were right, the total effect graceful, and I have never seen a sailboat with so little draft that was drier or abler. The deck came aft far enough to make a cuddy for gear and fishing tackle and it was possible for a man to tuck head and shoulders into it on the rare occasions when we sailed to distant harbours; though it was not to be recommended as a permanent berth. The mast was stepped through the deck, and on one of these boats was so far forward that our rig was a cat-lug. That is to say, the mainsail was the only sail and was made with a gaff but no boom. Its peak could be set up much higher than was possible with the old spritsail. The gaff was sometimes rigged with a leather-lined collar instead of jaws; and the sail could either be lowered into the boat and furled to the gaff, or by releasing the peak halliards only could be furled to the mast with the throat standing, though it was advisable to slack this halliard a little to avoid stretching in the wet. It was an extraordinarily convenient and effective rig, perfectly adapted to fishing on the reefs where a boom would have been an intolerable nuisance when the boat was at anchor or under oars; though in point of fact we took to oars only as a last resort in dead calms or when in light weather it became necessary to escape a hostile tide. There was later an adaptation of this rig on a slightly larger boat which set the mast further aft with a bowsprit and jib forward and even added, strange as it may seem, a small club topsail which gave good service when reaching or running in light airs, but involved too much rigging to make it advisable in so small a boat. These things were not of my devising but issued from the ingenious mind and deft hands of my frequent companion and most intimate boyhood friend for whom both boats had been built.

This young man was enough older than I to make his friendship of high value as well as deep satisfaction to me. Our close companionship continued until the width of the continent separated us and the friendship continues still, though he is dead. He was a better boatman than I because naturally quicker and defter though thanks to his example I soon became competent enough; and for years we ranged the woods, the marshes, the reefs, and the more distant waters to the south and east in as wholesome and rewarding adventure as ever fell to the lot of developing youth.

Behold us starting before sunrise from a little wharf three quarters of a mile from the sea. Bluefish have been reported on the reefs which means that a time of year has arrived when a light northerly wind may be expected in the early morning. Running out of the winding creek was therefore an easy business and so was our arrival on the line of reefs that stretch southwestward from Cornfield Point like the remains of an old terminal moraine, as perhaps it is, through Middle Reef, Hen and Chickens, Crane's Reef toward Southwest Reef, and so up-Sound indefinitely. It was unusual in my boyhood for large blue-fish to come to these reefs though of late years there has been a recurrence of them. Cornfield Point offered no strike at our trailing jigs, nor did the deeper water of Middle Reef, best of our blackfish grounds, nor the neighbourhood of Hen and Chickens where the fish-hawks built on the beacon long since replaced by a buoy. But to the westward on Crane's Reef there was hope. Fish were there. They were ready for breakfast; they began to strike; and we made a catch. It was not one to boast of either in numbers or in size, for they were but three-pound fish and not very many. Yet they are remembered for half a dozen reasons that make it worth while to set the memory down: for the beauty of a late summer morning; for the swift run to sea in bracing air; for the long swell sweeping over Crane's Reef that told of recent wind on the Ocean to the eastward; for the good companionship; for the mild excitement that even three-pound fish can provide; for the solid satisfaction of a decent catch even though one could not boast of it; for the pleasure of the return under easy sail; and for the general sense of drowsy well-being that flavoured the remainder of a day begun so early and auspiciously.

There were larger attempts. Days come back which saw us on the way to Fisher's Island and the Race; when we went ashore to cook supper in Little Hay Harbour (as we called it) without thought of trespass scarce dreaming of the time when to land on any shore of this happy refuge without permission might prove impossible; when we fished the Race on the next morning's tide though with but moderate success, and sought refuge on the flood under the lee of Race Rock where blackfish and flounders came up to greet us in rewarding numbers. On another day and with an ampler purpose we started for Fort Pond Bay with August at its best. The northerly breeze that means August at its best carried us across the Sound, through Plum Gut, and left us floating round the long sand-spit which Gardiner's Island thrusts from its south-western extremity. Then came the southerly wind setting us pleasantly along by the harbour of Napeague toward the Bay and its hospitable fish-house. This was in the keeping of a man from our north shore whom we knew and who added to his other accomplishments the gift of cooking not merely acceptably but with most appetising skill. Fish, fritters, pies, and cake — everything that went to the making of fine miscellaneous feeding came happily from his hand when, as was not always the case to be sure, he had the 'makings' of them. He lived much alone in such places as this, was reputed to have read the Bible through in one period of exile, had his peculiarities like most semi-hermits and was said once to have rushed into the fish-house, seized his gun, run out, and fired both barrels at a target that no one could discern. On inquiry it appeared that a wasp had annoyed him and he had thus waged loud and exterminating war upon it. At times he was subject to nightmare, and if memory serve me aright it was on the occasion of this visit that he partook of a cucumber and a cold clam fritter just before retiring with somewhat tempestuous results for us as well as him; but we brought him through.

Those unaccustomed to these boats might well have thought us foolhardy to attempt so long a voyage in so small a craft and to fish as we did on this occasion off Montauk, with an ocean swell sweeping in that hid the world when we went into the trough of it. I well remember that once all I could see of a passing schooner was her top-hamper from the cross-trees up; and I am ready to admit that such an excursion would have little appeal today.

But in point of fact the long swell held no danger so long
as it was lazy and there was water enough to keep it from
growing steep and breaking. Indeed on that cruise I do
not think we shipped a drop of water except the slop and
spray that we ourselves stirred up when threshing to windward in a brisk westerly breeze on the way home.

Fort Pond Bay and Montauk were places to see and
long remember in those halcyon days. The Bay was too
open toward the north but offered shelter from every other
wind; and held water that would almost let a schooner run
ashore at its head and permit a man to drop from the end
of her jib-boom to the beach. Even then there was talk
of its use as a terminal for ocean passenger traffic. The
land was wild, and almost unsettled save for a shanty near
the Point, the lighthouse, the Life-Saving stations on the
south shore, the fish-house where we stayed, and a shack
not far away in which dwelt an old negro who kept two
pigs for company as well as pork and whose single room
was black as ebony from the smudge with which in summer he fought mosquitoes. For these were undeniably
there and in such numbers when nights were close and
windless as to prove a serious obstacle to perfect enjoyment of the wilderness.

Not very long ago I visited the Bay again on a steamer
that made daily trips from New London. We ran up to
the head of the noble harbour to disembark passengers
and I looked about me with dismay murmuring 'Ichabod,
Ichabod'; for the glory had indeed departed. Railways incline to ugliness; but the Long Island Railroad had surpassed its kind. A sort of ragged terminal without apparent scheme, order, or proportion had usurped the head of
the Bay. Across the neck of land that separates the Bay
from the Ocean rose the absurdest structure that I think

even New York ever conceived and executed; for there dominating what used to be such pleasant wilderness, as assertive as the proverbial sore thumb, stood up a 'sky-scraper' — a ridiculous office building for which there must have been as little excuse as for a 'filling-station' on the outermost of the Hebrides. That there might be business demanding office work and a building to house it as the pestiferous land development went on I quite admit; but why anyone should have wanted to insult Heaven and spoil a naturally wild and lovely landscape by such a structure passes my seeing. It fits in, however, with the commercialisation which has laid a withering hand on so much of the southern New England countryside and which has led me to set down these memories before things that once were real shall seem quite incredible. Little is left of the friendly loneliness that the gunner and fisherman so often found upon our coast. So far as this means that more people can gain access to the shore one ought to be thankful rather than repine. But when one sees what once were pleasant fields desolated by helter-skelter shanties, and beaches crowded by multitudes who often act as though they cared more for the crowding than the sea, certain wistful memories of other days that at least seemed better will recur.

If space permitted I could tell at length how a great autumn gale once shut a boatman with my brother and myself into Napeague while boats big and little went ashore up and down the coast; how we made fast to a pier on the weather side of that pleasant harbour and held snugly on; how morning found the boat beside us blown away but without serious result, since it would be hard for any wind to blow a boat out of Napeague; how I was taken to see a poor woman with a terribly disordered hand which required immediate surgical attention; and how her husband started with her for Amagansett as soon as practicable after the gale. I took a 'land-tack' with them in a ramshackle wagon in order to catch a steamer in Sag Harbour and meet engagements on the mainland, leaving the others to bring the boat when the northwest gale which followed the southeaster should permit. Doubt soon oppressed me as to whether we should catch the stage that was to convey me from Amagansett to Sag Harbour, and the doubt seemed confirmed when, as we approached the entrance to the village, the old horse stumbled, lowered his head as if for a summersault, and almost turned one. Hope for the stage vanished. We disembarked expecting to find that a broken neck had finished our steed. But suddenly the worst turned to best. The horse survived his acrobatics and was pulled to his feet again; the woman I hope got the relief that she needed from the village doctor, though to a layman's eye it looked ominously like a case for amputation; and I caught my steamer after all — not only caught it but had an admirable chance to see what a mighty northwester could do when meeting the force of flood tide in Plum Gut. I had gone forward on the upper deck to stand in the shelter of the wheel-house and see what I might, knowing well that Plum Gut would be in a fine twitter. It was, and almost the first sea as the steamer struck the rip threw such a deluge over and around the wheel-house that despite my readiness for it I barely escaped a drenching.

When engines came in of course we could better determine the times of our going and coming. It was possible to intercalate a brief expedition between engagements on shore as one could not venture to do in the days of sail, though we lost something of the sense of outwitting nature and making a wind that wanted to hold us back really take us home; for the man who invented working to windward and getting on by means of opposing force gave almost an ultimate illustration of the conquest of matter by mind. I still remember a gorgeous August night when I tried to catch a half-hour's sleep on a heap of fishing gear amid the aggressive rats of a shanty beside the Connecticut while waiting for a ferryman to come off duty that we might start together for the other side of the Sound with the hope of bluefish in the morning. The moon was almost at its full and rode high in a cloudless sky as we ran out of the River about midnight. It was the time when both eastern and western night traffic concentrated in those waters, and a man who drowsed at the wheel invited disaster. One good-sized yacht illustrated the fact as she swept up-Sound at a roaring pace. Our courses converged and I had the right of way. But the skipper of a fishing boat is exceedingly ill-advised to stand too long upon the letter of the law when meeting a much larger and far swifter craft that may not have seen him at all or may see him quite too late. It was interesting that night to note the simultaneity of judgement on the yacht's bridge and in the cockpit of our boat. For just as I concluded that the safe distance for manoeuvring was reaching its limit and swung to port showing my green light, I saw the yacht's light quiver as its skipper reached the same conclusion, then swing back upon its course as though gratefully acknowledging the concession that I offered. I had been seen and my right of way would have been respected; but there is truth in the somewhat profane remark of an automobile passenger to a driver who had clung to the letter of the law until a collision was imminent, that he was claiming a 'right of way to Hell.' The secret of safety on both

land and sea lies in acting with a clear mind and acting,
above all, *in time.*

We reached a little cove at the western end of Plum
Island in time to lie down for forty winks, rose before
dawn to snatch a sort of pre-breakfast, got under way
and were in the Sluice to the south of the Island by the
time it was light. This was none too soon, for while between dawn and sunrise we took about thirty good fish,
after the sun came up I think not one. The sunrise was
memorable, so cloudless and brilliant in the cold morning
air (I was in sea boots and oilskins and needed them for
warmth as well as dryness) that I instinctively took off my
cap to his advent as though I had been a Persian. Then we
went back to the little cove, our well boiling with the swimming fish, drank our morning coffee, drew in close under
the Light among rocks that I should have avoided but for
the gentle easterly air setting us off from them, and in the
eddy formed by the mighty flood tide added nearly a
score of golden-brown blackfish to our catch, and were
back in the Connecticut soon after noon, dividing fish
among men, women, and cats and feeling in every fibre
of our sleepy beings the truth of

> Something attempted, something done,
> To win a night's repose.

Safe to say we had it with a lasting memory added thereto;
and if our month had been monosyllabic I should like to
have quoted in its behalf Browning's ascription to

> May's warm, slow, yellow, moonlit summer nights: —
> Gone are they, but I have them in my soul!

All things must conclude, even reminiscences of fishing;
but not until I have served the better wine at the feast's
end. Here I am prepared to be jeered at and told that my

better wine is in reality but the smallest of beer; yet I
cannot close this chapter without some specific reference
to the joys of bottom fishing. There are some who suppose
it to be merely the last resort of the man who can find no
other kind. I do not think so. Maine, Nova Scotia, Colorado, with the rivers and lakes of distant Newfoundland
have all paid me tribute. The deep-sea banks far beyond
Nantucket have shown me some fish; the Caloosahatchee
in Florida and the limpid coral depths of Bermuda have
shown me more. But after all, the reefs of Long Island and
Fisher's Island Sounds with occasional excursions into
those of the Vineyard and Nantucket have shown me most.
It is quite true that the man who knows this kind of bottom fishing only from the experience of an occasional day,
who has very likely found that day to be one of bad
weather, who has anchored as we have to anchor in the
edge of rips that are a little rough when the tide runs strong
and very rough when the wind blows, who has endured a
queasy stomach and perhaps paid Neptune the tribute he
so often demands for trespass, who has been disgusted
with the tiresome need of frequent hauling of lines to see
that bait is in good condition whether worth-while fish
bite or not, has seen other men catch fish while he
took none, or possibly sat through one of those rare but
still occasional days when the most experienced take little
or nothing — that such a man finds bottom fishing tiresome and will none of it when he can get something else, I
do not wonder. He naturally thinks that bluefishing is
better; and for a brief time on very occasional days it is.
But in the long intervals there is such a world of aimless
cruising, or a hurried rush to a point where fish have been
seen only to find that they have been driven down by the
greedy owner of some speed-boat whose aim in life is

merely 'to get there first.' Time after time he goes and
comes home with an empty well; or again with two or
three fish; and only on rare occasions does his well boil
and his cockpit show a carpet of scales. I am not decrying
bluefishing; but simply painting a portrait with the wrin-
kles and the occasional wart that Cromwell asked for.
Heaven forbid that I should decry any fishing unless it be
of the Caloosahatchee tarpon type where one is told to
mark the pool in which a tarpon has leaped, cast a bait
which he can swallow, and then fight a fish that is doomed
whether he come to the gaff or break away. That has
never appealed to me.

The reef-fisherman is probably after blackfish (*Tautoga
Americana* or *onitis*) sea-bass or cod. Let us state the case
against ourselves and suppose it to be blackfish. He is
but a commonplace comrade at the table, though not to
be despised, and in a chowder made by one who knows
capable of a quite memorable toothsomeness; and he is
far gamier than the occasional fisherman realises. Daniel
Webster used to catch him and might very fairly have
revised his famous tribute to Dartmouth to suit Tautoga's
case — a humble fish, but there are those who love him.

The interest of the reef-fisherman begins with the problem of bait. In the old days we used to catch blue crabs
with punt and scoop-net, make them drop their big claws,
and put them in ventilated 'cars' in the creeks beside our
boats where they would live indefinitely. And here at
once the fisherman learns something which many who
think themselves salt-water-wise never discern as he makes
gain of the ability of these crustaceans to drop a claw when
they wish and grow another. They will kill one another if
confined fully armed. But if the armed claw be struck
sharply at the elbow with a tiller or fid the crab can throw

the whole thing off at the shoulder without the slightest
wound. It is as though a door were simply taken off the
hinges. Thus the disarmed crabs become pacifist in their
own despite. Yet, as pacifists should consider in larger
matters, their hearts are not changed and if set at liberty
they grow a new set of weapons and eat one another up as
gaily as ever. In captivity this power is rarely exercised
however.

Perhaps the bait is the small green rock-crab to be
found under stones and enticed to baits in the creeks, or
the delicately constituted and beautifully mottled sand-
crab that must be used the day he is caught and that
squeaks a protest when the net deposits him in the boat.
The clear water of the outer sand flats is his playground
when the flood is making; and I have picked up a mess of
these on the young flood, gone at once to one of the nearer
reefs, caught a decent mess of fish, and come home on the
last of the same tide, all in a pleasant summer afternoon;
and he who thinks an afternoon spent thus alone in summer sunshine and sweet weather is not conducive to present content and future happy memories but half realises
his own resources.

I counted up the other night about forty of these
grounds that I had fished, more than four fifths of them
within five miles either of Cornfield Point or of the outer
New London Light. Let us try one of the former group.
Our boat is a small one, either a Hurlburt boat such as
has been already described or a plain sharpie that can be
handled under sail or oars. The crabs are already caught
and waiting in their car. A half-peck of clams has been
provided in case cunners prove too plentiful to waste
crabs on; and it may be that we have a few periwinkles —
very useful when fish are really hungry; or a little store of

hermit crabs — that 'ambiguous fish' of which Browning
sang. The reef is perhaps two and a half miles from our
moorings in the creek, but with the ebb running this distance can be quickly made. And here to begin with appears one of the worth-while things about reef fishing.
Tides must needs be studied, not merely the times of high
and low water, but the force that the flood will develop
when a third of it is run and the probable thickness or
clearness of the water on a neap or a spring tide; for phases
of the moon play a great part in this sort of fishing, and
apogee and perigee are words to conjure with. Now there
is nothing on the reef whither we are bound to show its
location to the landsman beyond a more or less defined
rip; and as the water has some depth this rip is not very
noticeable unless there is wind. Then indeed the landsman discovers it to the confusion of his stomach. Nor are
we to fish this reef in general. We are to find one particular spot upon it scarcely bigger than one's bedroom at
home and anchor so that our hooks will reach its immediate vicinity, due allowance being made for the force and
direction of both tide and wind. How? By ranges, of
course. When the kitchen chimney of a distant summer
hotel bears over a sharp-pointed rock a half-mile away and
just outside Cornfield Point, our east-and-west line is
established; and when to the north the upper left hand
corner of the doorway of a long barn rests in the notch of
an old pepperidge tree growing on a rocky knoll near the
beach a mile or two distant, the other range is true. Where
these two imaginary lines cross there will be found five-
and-twenty feet below (more or less) a very rough bit of
rocky bottom with a sharp peak in its midst that has cost
me more fishing tackle and perhaps yielded me more fish
than any other spot in the Cornfield Point area.

The reader will wonder that I should so recklessly and magnanimously set down the ranges of this ground, for fishermen are proverbially close-mouthed about their favourite nooks and corners. I like to be thought magnanimous; but the sad fact is that the hotel has been burned and never rebuilt, the barn has been pulled down, the pepperidge destroyed. Only the sharp-pointed rock outside the Cornfield bluff remains and even that is covered at high water; and it would require a range-finder based on something more than the geometry of Euclid to determine the locality with but one point given and neither distance nor direction exactly determined. I could find it again but not without effort and the recalling of other and less exact ranges, combined with some wearisome soundings. It is not that I grudge the knowledge, especially since relatively few 'summer fishermen' will ever take the pains even if they develop the skill to use it. For one of the satisfactions of this type of fishing lies just here. It is a pleasant game to determine one's ground by such distant means, making due allowance all the while for wind and current. I took a young man to one of these grounds some years ago. We were in his boat; but when the reef was reached I took the helm to get the ranges and 'lay her on,' and afterward heard that he told another fisherman who was a friend of mine of the strange fastidiousness of the helmsman; how he ran up on one course but seemed dissatisfied, turned instead of anchoring and made a second trial looking first in one direction and then in another, and it was not until several evolutions had been performed that this pernickety person was content to let his grapnel go. 'Yes,' replied the fisherman, 'but when you did finally anchor you caught fish, didn't you?' Which had to be admitted.

There are some grounds like the Champion and Darrow areas off New London or the Middle Ground to the south-westward of North Dumpling Light on which there is a chance of finding fish by what might be called 'anchoring in general'; but even here the wise fisherman will note his ranges whenever he feels good bottom or has a successful morning and go back to them. There are other grounds of quite different type; one in particular where a flat-topped rock shows just awash at low water near the land on one side while a relatively shallow but tide-swept reef lies on the other. The trick is to fish the reef on the last of the ebb and the young flood; then when the flood has grown until it begins to stir the sand and thicken the water to go in to that rock in a small boat, anchor so that its stern is in the wash of the waves running over the rock itself and with a fairly long rod explore its base. I have had excellent luck there sometimes sinfully enhanced by the fact that neighbours on the near-by reef were taking nothing. Once an experienced professional fisherman was the victim of this contrast which was heightened by a boat-load of boys to whom he was showing some fishing with very little success while the two or three boys over the rock were doing very well. But let me hasten to add that I too have had some of my own worst days when most anxious to show a friend how the thing was done and help him do it.

What are the fish that these reefs yield? I have called the roll of most of them in the chapter on the Farmer-Fisherman, since first and last specimens of all are likely to appear in the 'pounds' though none of those we catch were a principal object of the shad companies. On the shallower grounds together with the blackfish are to be found the ever-present and often vexatious cunner — the mosquito of the reefs — the northern flounder, the flat-fish, and now and then a sculpin representing the Gurnard family that finds its way far beyond the Arctic Circle. A rock cod may come along and is always welcome; but it is in the deeper water that we expect his bigger brother when the frosty days of autumn come in. There too in late summer the lovely little scup with his silver sides, bright eye, and narrow belly (*Chrysops stenotomus* is his name, remember) will appear in rewarding numbers, some-times a chiquit or weakfish will be caught and is worth holding up head forward so that one may see the pleasant foolish face of him with one sharp conical tooth (there are sometimes two) in the middle of the upper jaw. Very in-effectual this looks for any possible purpose of mastica-tion, as indeed it is, yet most helpful none the less for de-taining the active little neighbour who may endeavour to wriggle out of his engulfing mouth. The sea-bass is re-ceived with cheers and the striped bass would be if he were caught; but only on very occasional days does he feed deep enough or on such rocky bottom as to mingle with Tautoga.

Skates big and little join the company as now and then do the funny little swell-fish swallowing hard and puffing themselves into ludicrous rotundity. Twice I have caught a lobster on the hook and a few years ago found something weighing down my tackle that came up so heavily and slowly as to suggest the warp of an abandoned lobster pot. Looking curiously down I discerned at first a dim roundish outline that led me to wonder whether an ex-traordinarily meek and heavy flounder were not yield-ing to an influence that puzzled him. Still the object slowly rose until I recognised not the mere outline of a head but the long round body that went with it. He too had eyes to see, and as we recognised each other all the quietness of his coming vanished and he started up-Sound with a vigour that nothing could gainsay; for a hundred-and-fifty-pound shark (and he might easily have weighed so much) has a strength that no ordinary black-fish tackle can cope with especially when, as was probably the case with this fish, he is not hooked in the mouth but in the edge of the lip or possibly in the side. The creature felt little or no hurt in this case — merely a steady tug to which he yielded from a sort of curiosity; that satisfied and fully, we parted company.

Sometimes our fish come readily and steadily; sometimes they refuse to come at all. But for all that the experienced fisherman rarely returns without a 'mess' of something. Now and then a day has come to me when alone upon the reefs in heat or wind, when things have gone wrong in general, when tackle has fouled the bottom irrecoverably, when one's back has been well-nigh broken hauling anchor lines and shifting ground, while fish have consistently refused to bite. Then for an hour on getting home, wet, tired, and hungry, I may have wondered like Sam Weller struggling with the alphabet whether so much exertion paid; but, and this is the crucial test, I never woke next morning in any doubt or hesitation about it. The French have the true motto for the traveller to the effect that one never arrives until the next day. It is the morning's waking to a new scene rather than the weary outlook of a journey's end that tells the true story; and it is so with fishing.

Time fails me to tell of my companions, preferably one at a time in a boat, since fishing is no business for a noisy or careless group. It is a business to be gone about discreetly, soberly, and in the fear of God. Then it yields

memorable rewards and quiet confidences that enhance
the treasures of life. I have fished with highly cultivated
men and with the plainest of boatmen and profited by
both. Good weather is to be preferred for the former,
when talk can range at its will and there is little hard sea
work to be done. When wind comes up, seas rise, or fog
shuts down it is helpful to have resourceful practical companionship especially since boats have grown so much
larger and heavier as often to demand the strength of
two.

It is idle to attempt the listing of the rewards of all this
going to and fro upon the sea. One man may feel the richest of them in quiet summer weather when fish are biting
with reasonable appetite, when sea and land are bright
in sunshine and the fisherman watches the play of pleasure
boats, the business of working craft, the distant crowds
on some bathing beach just within his view. For myself
the autumn fishing claims first place. The sea is lonelier;
but the land takes on new beauty as the pepperidge and
poison sumac begin to light their lamps; or later still the
maples and oaks in the woods and the heaths of the open
pastures brighten the world. Then as one turns homeward perhaps out of the grip of a sea that has knocked
boat and crew about since morning, and with which his
oilskins still shine in the beams of a watery sun, or quite as
likely in a peace even lovelier than that of midsummer as
the world enters upon that 'truce and sabbath of the year'
which October and November sometimes offer — then
he thanks God for salt water and catches himself murmuring, 'The sea is His, and He made it.'

XI

The Church in the Village

THERE is a legend not to be lightly dismissed as unhistorical that some of the chief leaders of Parliament in its struggle with Charles I for constitutional rights actually went on board ship with a view to emigration, John Hampden and Oliver Cromwell with them. Hume among Tory writers and Nugent among Whig historians credit the story. So does Robertson; and so do sundry of their commentators and critics. I think it open to grave doubt rather than quite disproved. But there is no doubt at all that several of these leaders, Lord Say and Lord Brooke among them, gave serious thought to emigration. Vane and Saltonstall actually came to New England. Had the crucial year, 1637, passed into history with a slightly different outcome Say, Brooke, and Hampden might have emigrated. An attempt had been made to prepare a place for them at the mouth of the Connecticut and to it they would pretty certainly have come. It had been named for the two peers and bears their names today. The scheme for an aristocratic society even with such liberal Lords and Gentlemen as these for its upper class could scarcely have succeeded at Saybrook or elsewhere in the new and raw colonial life of that first decade.

Yet the half-attempt is worth recording for a number of reasons.

Among these is the religious one. Hume with characteristic cynicism speaks of Hampden and his followers as moved toward emigration to New England by their desire for sermons seven hours long. Lord Nugent in those Memorials of Hampden that Macaulay reviewed so notably a century ago in the 'Edinburgh Review' quotes this remark and proceeds to argue against Hume's statement not only on the ground of its general absurdity but because these men were Independents (or Congregationalists) instead of Presbyterians; and it was the latter rather than the former who could stomach long sermons. How extended Presbyterian patience may be I do not pretend to say; but I am prepared to state without much fear of contradiction that Congregational patience was likely to be worn out much more quickly than we have been wont to suppose.

The matter is worth mention because it illustrates the animus that has characterised so much of the treatment of New England by 'literary persons' and by some historians. The early settlers of New England have been unwisely and sometimes extravagantly praised. They have been as unwisely and perhaps even more extravagantly slandered. The lamentable hysteria of Salem witchcraft for example has been treated as though it were so outstanding an instance of superstitious fear as to be almost unique, and as though its cruelty were sadistic instead of incidental; as though, too, the bad business belonged by special right to the Puritan habit and character; whereas in point of fact the blood shed in America was but a drop in comparison with the flood which reddened the map of Europe in Catholic and Protestant countries alike on the same sad account; and in New England, moreover, the craze was as brief as it was bad. The intelligence of educated men asserted itself and the cure proved permanent; though in England and Scotland persecution lingered on at least to 1727. Nor can I quite understand why Cotton Mather's lamentable part in it should be so steadfastly remembered as characteristic while his valiant sponsorship of inoculation for smallpox maintained against a deal of popular prejudice should be forgotten.

The Puritan has also been again and again pictured as delighting in cruel punishments and enacting a barbarous code of laws. In point of fact when the laws of the Connecticut Colony were codified and this town of Saybrook became subject to them about a dozen crimes — I think exactly twelve — were punishable by death; while a century later even in supposedly enlightened England one hundred and sixty-four offences were liable to that penalty, and the number gradually increased until, about the time when Romilly began his humane protests, it had grown to two hundred and over. Incidentally, the reader of the early history of Massachusetts as he encounters instances of heavy fines assessed needs to keep in mind the many cases in which they were actually remitted. Who has not been fed *ad nauseam* with the story of the man who returned from sea on a Sunday morning, kissed his wife, and, the embrace being observed, was fined for it? We may be sure enough that men might kiss their wives when moved to do so on Sundays as on other days, but that public displays of affection, especially when of too suggestive a character, were frowned upon. It is safe to say that the ancestors of folk so generally credited with hard sense as the Yankees were not themselves entirely destitute of the quality. Only as one looks beneath the

surface does it appear how often some exceptional incident, sometimes as exceptional then as now, has been
used as the basis of a too general conclusion. Several men,
for instance, in 1656, were brought before the Particular
Court in Hartford for smoking on the streets and pre-
sumably either warned or fined. It is however the only
instance that I have discovered in the annals of the
Court's first twenty-five years, and it may well be unique
in its history. Yet some day an historian of colonial manners and morals will almost certainly cite it as normal.

These men have often been characterised as unfeeling
and quite bereft of humour. Yet Margaret Winthrop's
letters to her husband breathe an affection as deep as it
was constant. Once she sets forth some reasons why she
loves him and begins 'First because thou lovest God and
secondly because thou lovest me.' Mrs. Winthrop the
younger one day went about some needle-work or dress-
making task with pins in her mouth and the Governor of
Massachusetts writes to the future Governor of Connecticut: 'My good Son, I received your letter and do heartily
rejoice and bless the Lord for his merciful providence toward us all in delivering your wife from so great a danger.
The Lord make us truly thankful. And I hope it will
teach my daughter and other women to take heed of putting pins in the mouth which was never seasonable to be
fed with such morsels.'

The plain fact is that these people can never be understood without reference to their religion. That has been
recognised. The further fact that this religion had a
serious and sometimes a stern aspect has not only been
recognised, but so overemphasised as often to give an entirely jaundiced and distempered picture of their thought
and life. Eliot, the Apostle to the Indians, was not only a

man of devoted life but of happy and humorous disposition. Shepard of Cambridge was always enlivening the
most solemn subjects with the play of a sprightly mind.
Even when a man took the formulas and rituals of religion
so seriously as to be cantankerous about them he was
sometimes able to show a high and even gracious generos-
ity in practical affairs. Roger Williams of blessed memory
is an outstanding example. There was apparently a time
when he was unable to commune with anybody beyond
the borders of his own family; and one wonders whether
the orthodoxy of his much-enduring wife were not under
occasional suspicion. He was, indeed, one of the most con-
tentious of men in respect of theory. Yet he took his life
in his hand to visit the Narragansett chiefs on the eve of
the Pequot War; and it is scarcely too much to say that
his success in holding them to their neutrality saved the
little Saybrook Colony and the settlements about Hartford from annihilation. It was a magnanimous exhibition
of practical brotherly service that covers a multitude of
doctrinal squabbles. So with many others. Their faults
were not only plentiful but manifest; and the tendency of
too many historians has been to make these faults normal
and regulative of the entire social and religious life of the
people.

Now it has been my lot to know intimately a large number of persons who stood in the direct Puritan line with
respect to their religious and ethical beliefs and the conduct issuing from them. They were village people; they
were attendant upon and many of them members of the
village Church; they cherished, some with great affection,
some with less, its faith and traditions; and I am bound to
say that upon the whole this inheritance seemed to be one
of the most beneficent features of their individual and
corporate life.

This Church was an ancient one as that word is understood in America. It was not so old as the settlement because for some years this was a military post and the colonists were served by chaplains of the fort. But two hundred and ninety years ago the people met, probably in the Fort's Great Hall; an organisation was effected; a young minister was ordained; and the corporate life of the Church began. It has never been intermitted; its worship has never ceased; its testimony to the 'things of the Spirit' has never lapsed. I do not say that it has done its whole duty or lived up to its ideal. There have been periods of decline and other times of awakened and awakening life. But year in and year out, through good times and bad, it has never failed to proclaim what it believed to be a gospel. The 'literary person' usually makes this 'gospel' to consist in a preaching of fire and brimstone and an attempt to frighten men into the acceptance of a grim and impossible creed. Well, it is the privilege of 'literary persons' to do this. The late 'Elmer Gantry' illustrated the general tendency to caricature religious folk and folkways. He represents them, as an intelligent critic remarked at the time of his appearance, very much as the old-time coloured valentine exploited the folk at whom it was aimed. It was unfair, to be sure; but when did novelists of Mr. Sinclair Lewis's type ever desire or endeavour to be fair? Prejudice is a chief weapon in their arsenals; and one must try to be patient and good-tempered toward their pleasure in brandishing it. The deep-seated and sometimes virulent prejudice of so excellent an historian as Mr. Truslow Adams is a far more serious matter. But something must be allowed to personal idiosyncrasy and it is better even here to bear with this as 'pretty Fanny's way.'

I am far from wishing to seem contemptuous of the learning and services of Mr. Adams. But his picture of the early New England clergy as a parcel of malignants will not bear close examination, and his later picture of the 'industrial revolution' seems to me to lack perspective. It is painted in the drab and sometimes tragic colours of the large industrial centres like Lowell. I do not recall a single reference to the great number of relatively small industries, each in its New England village, that brought new opportunity to thousands of village folk; or to the little shops that so often stood beside New Hampshire homesteads suggesting the piece-work that came to many families in their dull season from the neighbouring shoe factories. It was very likely inadequately paid for as has generally been the case with cottage piece-work; but it brought in cash and shortened the long winters when remunerative outdoor work was scarce.

I wonder too if Mr. Adams ever heard of the journey to New England of Doctor Scoresby, the famous Arctic explorer and authority on terrestrial magnetism. He was that *rara avis* a scientific man of distinction who was at the same time deeply interested in social welfare; and he came to Lowell from England to study the steps taken to benefit the social life of the mill-workers in hope that similar efforts might be made in the English mills. It was in 1844. Whether this reflects credit on the Lowell mill-owners or discredit on those of Yorkshire and Lancashire I do not undertake to say; but the journey is a fact worthy of mention.

Let us return from this digression to our Church. That little congregation which gathered on Sundays and Lecture Days for worship and instruction has an interest for the country at large out of all proportion to its numbers or its wealth. The ancestors of two Presidents of the United States were probably there. Its first minister was one of the leaders of the later migration to Norwich. To his work among the Mohicans may be traced the Lebanon Indian School, out of which Dartmouth College finally developed, and the Oneida School, whose principal gave a president to Harvard. From one of the first deacons of this Church descended the first President of King's College, which has become Columbia University and the first President of Columbia itself. From another member of the same family descended Horace Bushnell with his singularly elevated influence upon education, religious thought, and civic life; and Cornelius Bushnell whose active support of Ericsson made the construction of the 'Monitor' possible in time to interrupt the 'Merrimack's' career and introduce a new era in naval warfare.

Mr. Buckingham, who ministered to the Church from 1665 to 1709, was active in rousing his parish to withstand the landing of Sir Edmund Andros in 1675 and in thwarting his design upon the Fort. Later he collaborated in founding the Collegiate School that developed into Yale College and University; he fostered its beginnings; the early meetings of its Trustees were probably held in his parsonage; while of the fifty-five graduates during the School's Saybrook life, nine were natives of his parish. He and two of his chief laymen were members of the Synod which met in Saybrook in 1708 to frame the Saybrook Platform, and project the ideals of that generation into the ecclesiastical order of the next century and a half; and one of his chief services to a far later day was in providing Connecticut with its competent and high-minded Governor, William A. Buckingham, who guided the affairs of the Commonwealth during the War between the States.

As one calls the roll of these ministers for the two-hun-
dred and ninety years of the Church's corporate existence,
no unworthy or false man appears among them. Some
were men of distinct light and power of leadership; some,
no doubt, were commonplace. Whatever they were it is
safe to say that the inquiring minds of a New England
village found them out. Almost without exception they
were men of intelligence, education, and character. One
man supplied the pulpit for a short time between two pas-
torates whose abilities — and they were real enough —
won much acceptance and probably inclined some toward
his call. But investigation into his antecedents cast such
grave doubt upon character and conduct that all thought
of this was abandoned. It was the only time, so far as
records or memory go, that the light of this Church
seemed likely to prove a will-o'-the-wisp. There were
times when it glowed like a beacon; times when it sunk to
relative feebleness; but it was always a light of life which
if followed led to a more nearly perfect day.

I suspect that one of the chief services of the Church,
next at least to its immediate influence upon the current
day with its duties and its chances, has been in the sowing
of memories to bear fruit in future years. From 1783 to
1844 it was in charge of a remarkable man. The length
of his pastorate indicates that it was a life-charge. He
came as a youth of little more than twenty; he died as
Senior Pastor at the age of eighty-one. Strong, vigorous,
authoritative, evangelical, and kindly, he was a power in
the community; but he was far from being a tyrant.
Stories still linger of his shrewd and humorous rebuke of
slack farming or slovenly housekeeping as he noted them
in pastoral visitation. Some of his discourses remain to
testify against those who are forever decrying the fire

and brimstone which the sermons of his day are supposed
to breathe and the enormous length to which they are supposed to have run. In point of fact one of these that lies
nearest to my hand, though preached on a special occasion
that might have incited to length and also excused it, can
be easily read aloud in a half-hour. Little smell of fire is
on any page of those that I have seen. They speak rather
with strong conviction, deep though controlled affection,
and sound sense of those things of the Spirit which long
life and service had proved to possess abiding truth.
They called this man 'Father' Hotchkiss and the name was
well applied.

Long after his death I chanced to hear a scholarly and
experienced man read some reminiscences of him. Though
of kindly nature the reader was as far as possible from
being a sentimentalist. Indeed he was of such markedly
controlled and equable habit that during a somewhat intimate acquaintance I can recall but one instance in which
he showed visible emotion. This was the occasion of it.
As he read and as the long life of service unrolled itself
to his memory and strove to live again in his words his
utterance broke and it became for a moment uncertain
whether he could go on. A curious parallel to this happened when the late Professor G. P. Fisher of Yale under-
took one day to recall some characteristics of another New
England clergyman who stood distinctly in the Puritan
succession, albeit a progressive interpreter of Puritan doctrine. None who had the slightest acquaintance with
Professor Fisher needs to be told how far his learned,
keenly critical, and very humorous mind was from being
easily swayed by emotion. Never, in his lecture room, at
his table, or in his walks have I seen any sign of a struggle
for self-control except on one occasion — and again, this

was the occasion: he seemed to see once more a man who
had fostered his youth, a man of outstanding ability,
keen in his search for truth and warm in his love of it,
eagerly desirous to interpret it generously in terms fitted
to the life of his time, glad to plough his own works and
days into fields that were to feed the next generation;
and the vision for the moment rapt him out of his studied
and habitual calm until it shook his voice and filled his
eyes.

In the case of a later minister of godly life, scholarly
tastes, and good abilities the legend ran that at family
prayers he was wont to translate from the Hebrew or the
Greek of the Old and New Testaments while his wife used
a French and his elder daughter a Latin text. I cannot
vouch for the story though it is probable enough; but the
point is that the people liked it, not as a mere linguistic
feat, though that was pleasant, but as a sign that their
minister brought to his pulpit instruction, sound learning,
and a vision that went beyond the commonplace. Their
own lives were often necessarily circumscribed. But on
Sundays when they took their place in church the horizon
lifted. A larger stage than that of the common day was
set before them. The business of the common day very
likely kept its place there but it was illumined by a clearer
light; its values were related to higher issues; the experience of the Past was brought to the problems of the
Present; while the Present opened into a hopeful and possibly a blessed Future.

It is easy to say that this attendance was a matter of
form — a mere feature of the village *mores*. So no doubt
it was in the case of some; but in the case of many it was
as undoubtedly one of the most vital elements in their
cultural lives; and in 'cultural' I include not only the things

related to worship in the etymological meaning of 'culture,' but all that interweaving of the mental and spiritual, the ethical and social that made them what they
finally became.

There was one man, for instance, whose home was on a
farm in a remote section of the parish. It was distant from
neighbours as well as from town. He was a man of the
strictest integrity as well as of unresting industry. Had
he been complimented upon the latter trait he would
probably have ascribed it to necessity for his farm was not
very fertile, his distance from markets considerable, his
family of generous size, he was dependent upon it for such
help as he had and at the same time he and his wife were
ambitious for the education of their children. His eldest
son recently sketched to me this man's Sunday as he remembered it in the days of morning and afternoon service
when his father sat among the bass singers in the choir.
Of course there were morning chores to be got out of the
way and the evening chores to be arranged for. Clothes
were changed, the horse harnessed, the children gathered,
and the long drive to church accomplished. The morning
service was at half after ten; Sunday School followed as
near twelve as might be, and lasted an hour. Then people
separated for home and dinner, since the old days of the
little 'Sabba-day' houses in which lunch was eaten and
gossip exchanged had long passed by. It was not always
so for him. He marshalled his children and headed for
home, to be sure; but time and again the hour proved too
brief. He would then discharge the children at the foot
of a long hill on the crest of which his house stood, and
while they walked up he would turn back dinnerless in
order to take his place in the choir for afternoon service.
Then, when home was reached at four or something after,

one of the younger children would be lifted to his lap for
such instruction in spiritual things as his weariness could
manage. It is not to be wondered at that, invincible
though the spirit was in the campaigns of life, the flesh
sometimes won a skirmish and sleep overcame him before
the lesson had gone very far; and it is fitting that today
his memory should be kept green and his influence extended by a scholarship in one of the oldest endowed
schools of New England, of which his son was the successful headmaster.

I do not forget how generally the life of the Church as
pictured in current fiction becomes a sordid thing of pretence, narrow criticism, or narrower self-righteousness, of
meanness, and of faction. It is very far from my purpose
to represent it as realising its ideal. This Church of which
I am speaking was no circle of perfected saints. Yet in
the long run very few folk who could be branded as
hypocrites were to be discerned. Some of the most faulty
may well have been sincere in their search for forgiveness
and for strength in difficulty; and there was astonishingly
little to be gained by false pretences, since on the one
hand they could not long escape detection, and on the
other neither membership in the Church nor support of
it was a condition of worldly success. There were occasional unhappy and unchristian feelings between members,
but there was little sustained faction or bitterness. As
to fire and brimstone and the elaboration of abstruse doctrine, there might well have been a little more of the
former, for I cannot remember ever hearing a reference
to them in all my years of church attendance as a youth,
and Hell itself was mentioned a thousand times in ill-
advised speech upon the street to once in the pulpit;
which seems a pity because it is so much of a present

reality, whatever one's opinion of its future, that it were wiser to give some thought to its nature and its causes. Doctrine was not, I think, very often or very largely discussed; because when a doctrinal sermon was preached it seemed to excite remark, unfavourable if the treatment were dry but delightedly interested when great doctrines were made vital in terms of the common day and related to the struggles and possible triumphs of the individual life; for there is truth in Robert Louis Stevenson's remark that you can keep no men long nor Scotsmen at all from theological discussion. It is a truth to which the somewhat windy eloquence of the late Robert Ingersoll testifies as truly as does the undying — and generally misinformed — memory of Jonathan Edwards. Men do not, to be sure, commonly discuss the problems of the universe or of the soul around a card table or in a country club; but let intelligent and informed talk drift to the mysteries and practical problems of life's origin, conduct, and destiny and hearing ears will be opened.

An eminent and learned writer has recently remarked that 'no matter what figure one uses it takes life and vision, truth and faith, need and answer, the divine and the human to make any sermon. It is poor enough at its best ... sputtering with static at its clearest, but if it establish one brief contact between us and the Unseen and Eternal it has served its ends.' [1] This a multitude of the services of this Church did as was evidenced in the experience of a good many of us. Nor is the statement to be limited to the services or the parish of this ancient Church to which for historical reasons and those of personal acquaintance I have chiefly referred. There was a little preaching station

[1] G. G. Atkins, *Preaching and the Mind of Today.* (Round Table Press, New York, 1934), p. 200.

maintained by Methodists in one corner of the town; and there were two fully organised churches, one Roman Catholic which in the early days of my remembrance lacked a resident priest but which grew steadily in strength and influence, the other an Episcopal Church whose simple Gothic rose in stone during my boyhood and always pleased my eye, while its services and several admirable men among its ministers were of value to me as no doubt they were to others outside their immediate communion. I liked its ritual, its emphasis upon gradual spiritual culture as contrasted with the expectation of sudden and violent change — though it must be remembered that both find place in the religious life — and the link that it formed for the historically minded with the Mother Country; and it was no very unusual thing for members of our family to attend its services. There were of course small or prejudiced folk on both sides of the denominational fence who could more clearly discern the faults than the merits of each other, the Congregationalist emphasising what he thought to be the 'formalism' of his misguided brother, while the brother, certainly misguided now, retorted by writing his own Church with a very big 'C' and placing an even greater emphasis upon the littleness of the 'c' accorded to his neighbour, if indeed he did not insist upon referring to him as a member of a 'sect.' Now and then too someone whose prejudice surpassed her knowledge of history could be heard talking of 'Nonconformists' or 'Dissenters' — words which Connecticut and Massachusetts folk could dismiss with a smile.

But deeper than all this very occasional surface folly lay a sound mutual respect which I like to think deepened not infrequently into affection. Wise folk, and there were always such, realised the common nature of the tasks of both. One of the distinguished sons of the Episcopal Church, for many years Secretary of its House of Bishops, and of good Congregational ancestry be it noted, was a chief authority upon the history of the Town and of both Churches. Another Episcopal clergyman formerly of the staff of Grace Church in New York and united by marriage with one of the town's older families, brought to the three-hundredth anniversary of its settlement a fund of colonial lore, a gift for the happy portrayal of the past, a contagious enthusiasm, and a magnanimous unselfishness which will long be gratefully remembered by the Congregational clergy with whom he always co-operated and whom he often led.

One thing remains to be said with reference to the practical impact of the Church upon the life of the Village as a whole. It would be foolish to claim that any church did all it might have done for the social service of the community. It was not always ahead of its time in knowledge though it was forward-looking. But when questions of better schools, better roads, better public morals, cleaner politics, a more brotherly attitude toward folk disadvantaged by poverty, illness, disaster, or wrongdoing came up for solution the folk, who could be depended upon not merely for verbal or even for financial sympathy but for a steadfast support that had patience, took pains, and gave time and strength as well as mere assent, were usually to be found among the active members of these two parishes. I do not depend upon memory alone in saying this. The examination of a diary often referred to in these pages has impressed me with the sure and quick response which time and time again has followed the burning of a poor man's house, or some special inroad of illness, or the discovery of some unwonted pinch of individual or family poverty; and how surely among the leaders in efficient endeavour to meet the need were to be found those who had learned the privilege and duty of translating truth into goodness in these Christian Churches.

XII

Terminus a Quo

ONE often hears it said that New England is a province living so much to itself as to be oblivious of the remainder of the country; and particularly that it is ignorant as well as careless of the West. My own experience leads me to question that statement, which is after all more often uttered as a challenge than as a considered opinion. Like Scotland, New England has been obliged to look beyond her own boundaries for the means of livelihood. One of her principal crops has been men who have ploughed the sea on the one hand, and the plains, the rivers, and the lakes of the West on the other. These have generally retained some interested memories of their old home. Many have revisited it if only to show how well they have got on and to tell through what experiences they have passed. More have kept in at least partial touch with former friends by letter or newspaper and have handed on enough home tradition to their children to keep family interest alive.

Now it must be remembered that this interest is by no means a one-sided affair. It is reciprocated, vitally and heartily, by the East. Indeed anyone who really knows village life at first hand will be struck by the detailed information concerning parts of Iowa, let us say, or of South-

ern California to be found in some home whose owners
have never set foot beyond the Hudson. The very quiet
of their unadventurous lives has sent their minds afield;
about their daily tasks they have fed imagination with
vicarious travel; they have seen old friends as described
in their letters busied with the affairs of a strange if not
an alien soil. I well remember the call of a small farmer
whose daughter was in the employ of my family just as I
was about to start on a journey to the Near East. His
errand was merely to supply the larder with some product
of his farm. But the genuine earnestness with which he
expressed a hope that I might find time to write a few
letters to the local paper is still vivid. It was no mere
gesture of civility. The man had lived his life so far and
would in all probability live the remainder of it within call
of his morning and evening chores. Yet there was in him
something of the same urge to see the world that made the
poet Cowper, immured in his cottage and garden in Ol-
ney, such an avid reader of books of travel. Another small
farmer came once to my house in a Massachusetts city to
deliver his weekly supply of butter or eggs and explained
his coming at an unusual hour by the fact that he wished
to return home in time to attend the Oratorio to be sung
by a great chorus that afternoon; and he spoke as one to
whom music was a high concern. Now I have known as
narrow and sordid provincialism on a New England farm
as I have ever found anywhere, and much recent writing
about country life seems to imply that narrow and sordid
conditions are necessarily incident to it. No one can say
exactly how frequent the incidence is. What I am now
pointing out is the highly important sections of New England life that compelled the eyes of men and women to
look abroad.

Many a Maine housewife was as much at home sewing her children's clothes upon her husband's quarter-deck while running down the northeast trades or at anchor in a Mediterranean harbour as in her own living-room. It seems but yesterday that I stopped on the street to speak with a very old lady who had gone round the Horn to make a home in Chili or the Sandwich Islands for her husband then acting as factor there for shipping firms in Connecticut. She had taken the long journey and the considerable exile in her stride, so to speak, as she took the keeping of her New London house and the bearing of her children. I called the other day at a rather remote farmstead in the hills of mid-Connecticut. The man I went to see was now too old for active farming; but his windows opened upon acres that he had known since childhood and which one may well believe his eyes had longed to see again amid the darkness of Arctic winters; for he had spent a good part of his life in going up and down the seas of all the earth after whales with especial emphasis upon the difficult regions to the north of Hudson Bay. He knew Southampton Island, Sir Thomas Rowe's Welcome, Repulse Bay; he knew the Esquimaux as a race, as separate tribes, and in the persons of many individuals. He knew explorers, not merely as they appeared in print but as they were in person and character. It was quite in keeping with the subject of our talk that as we parted he should have given me a thin rod of teak about a yard long. There was nothing very distinctive about its look unless it were to some inlander to whom teak was a novelty. Yet the little ship of which it was a part had made history. She had been bought by Lady Franklin; had sailed into the ice under Captain (afterward Sir Leopold) McClintock; had been nipped in Baffin Bay and drifted helpless for a

winter; had turned with indomitable purpose when released back to the North again; had fought her way
through Lancaster Sound and down Prince Regent Inlet
to her winter quarters in Bellot Strait, whence McClintock
made some of the great sled journeys of Arctic history, in
them established the fate and from them brought back the
authentic relics of Sir John Franklin and his men. His
ship survived the expedition, passed into Danish hands
and the Greenland service, found her grave on the Greenland coast, and yielded from her abandoned hull this
memento to an East Haddam farmhouse.

Though quite aware that there is no need to labour this
wide outlook of many a new England village I cannot for-
bear mention that my windows look out to the hills of the
town whence came John Ledyard who abandoned Dartmouth College for the sea, accompanied Captain Cook
on his last and fatal voyage, attempted to cross Europe
and Asia from the Atlantic to the Pacific, actually making
his way into mid-Siberia before the Russians stopped him;
and finally died in Cairo while planning an African journey that he hoped might be continental in its scope.
The next town amid its rocky farms mothered Nathaniel
Palmer who while little more than a boy took the forty-
ton sloop 'Hero' to the South Shetlands on a sealing expedition, and then in search of new rookeries went so deep
into the Antarctic as to discover Palmer Land. This was
long supposed to be a part of the Antarctic Continent
proper and was so regarded by the Russian explorer Bellingshausen whose expedition Palmer encountered and who
gave him credit for anticipation in the discovery. It was
later found to be an archipelago in immediate conjunction
with what is now called Graham Land; and we of southern
Connecticut still feel it to be unhandsome of the geo-

graphers to have belittled Palmer's unquestioned discovery of a large archipelago by attaching his name to one
relatively insignificant island of it. He was, to be sure,
only a sealhunter and little more than a boy at the time;
but his voyage from Stonington to the Antarctic in a
forty-ton sloop was an achievement, the priority of his
discovery was recognised by the eminent Russian naviga-
tor, and Palmer himself grew to be a highly important
figure in world commerce by reason of the famous ships
that he not only designed but sailed to England, California, and China. It used to be said of him that he was perhaps the only man who ever had a great clipper ship, a
yacht, and part of a continent named for him.

Lyme Street still bears the impress of the captains who
built some of its houses; the Church so often painted by
artists and burned in 1907 was probably the work of ship-
carpenters when erected in 1816–17; and there is a tradition that its plans were brought from England by one of
the Griswolds. This is almost demonstrably not a fact
because we have copies of the contract with the master-
builder who erected it; but it is possible that some books
on architecture reflecting the influence of Christopher
Wren and his London Churches may have come through
that channel. In my boyhood the tang of the deep sea was
more closely associated with Essex than with Old Saybrook, her mother town, yet even there I was reminded by
the wooden statue of the Duke of Northumberland [1] up-
reared from the roof of Captain Leander Spencer's buildings that he had been master of a ship of that dignity and
had preserved her figurehead.

But humbler people than these shipmasters made history and helped to widen home-horizons.

---

[1] It may have been some other Duchy — Devonshire possibly; but at any
rate mouth-filling and sonorous.

There was in 1822 a boy in Saybrook, probably in the western part of town, by the name of William Lay. He heard the call of the sea and shipped on the whaleman 'Globe' which sailed from Nantucket in December for the Pacific Ocean, there to become the scene of one of the bloodiest mutinies in the annals of American or English seagoing. After taking a whale in the Atlantic, making a call at the Sandwich Islands, visiting the Japan Deep, and stowing about 550 barrels of oil, the 'Globe' returned to the Islands and there shipped a half-dozen desperate men to replace an equal number of deserters. These beach-combers found a congenial leader in one of the ship's boat-steerers named Comstock. His brutal and vindictive nature almost suggests homicidal mania, for there seems to have been no cruelty inflicted on the crew and no very serious cause of complaint beyond a somewhat inefficient management of the food supply, in which the sailors' jealously cherished meat was sometimes overabundant and sometimes scanty. On the way to Fanning's Island, under the leadership of Comstock with the Beach-comber Payne as his lieutenant, the mutineers murdered the Captain and all three of the mates with circumstances of the most horrid cruelty, cast their bodies overboard before life was in every case extinct, and steered for the Mulgrave Islands. Fortunately for such survivors as were out of sympathy with the mutiny the life of a competent boat-steerer named Smith had been spared. The reader must understand that the 'boat-steerer' was rated as a petty-officer whose duty it was to harpoon the whale, then to change places with the officer who was to lance and kill it, and to steer the boat during this process. Many of these men were acquainted with navigation and looked forward to command. On arrival at the Mulgraves the ship was

brought as close as possible to land with the view of dis-
mantling and burning her, as the mutineers treated the
'Bounty' at Pitcairn Island. Much was taken ashore.
But in the process the leaders quarrelled and Comstock
was killed. Soon after this Smith saw or made his chance;
recovered a binnacle compass secretly; went aboard before sundown; and when darkness fell managed with a
handful of companions to let the fore and main topsails
and the mainsail fall in the brails, to sever the forward
moorings with a greased saw, to cut the after hawser with
a hatchet as the ship fell off before the evening land breeze,
and, though pitifully shorthanded, to work her into distant Valparaiso.

There the authorities took their report in hand and
many months later a United States ship was sent to the
Mulgraves to apprehend the mutineers. Its commander
found as might have been expected that they had fallen
out among themselves as did the earlier mutineers on
Pitcairn, that they had given just cause of offence to the
natives, and that the latter had finally wrought judgement upon them by a general massacre. Which brings us
back to William Lay of Saybrook. He could scarcely have
been considered a mutineer nor could the other boy,
Cyrus Hussey of Nantucket. They simply had to yield
to the majority to save their lives; and some dim sense of
this seems to have penetrated the savage mind, for while
every mutineer perished these two were spared. It was by
a narrow chance, however, for Lay's life was threatened,
and would have been taken had not an old man and his
wife drawn him apart, sat down beside him, and held his
hands. He supposed himself to be the only survivor, but
learned to his joy a few days later that Hussey still lived.
They met for a brief interview, but separation soon fol-

lowed, and a captivity sometimes cruel and sometimes kind yet always hazardous and distressing continued until the latter part of 1825 when the armed schooner 'Dolphin' under the command of Lieutenant Commander John Perceval rescued them, rewarded the natives who had befriended them, and by transfer to the frigate 'United States' at Valparaiso set them on their way home. The story of their adventure was printed in New London and doubtless still awaits in some Connecticut attics the hand of the collector — a little brown leather-covered volume as full of authentic blood and thunder as any that I know. I have thought it worth somewhat extended mention here as showing that more than a century ago the quietest of seaport villages, so far from being cabined and confined, had eyes that saw around the world.

Nor was the landward view much less restricted. Neighbours have always been going West, young men to make their fortunes, middle-aged men with their families, old folk to find a milder climate for their age. At first of course 'West' meant central New York, then Ohio and Wisconsin, then the Great Plains beyond the Mississippi, then Texas and California. Scarcely a family but had some kinship with this wide and ever widening exodus. My own people were eminently home-lovers; but my Great-Grandfather had been to Canada in one of the expeditions against the French and later had commanded a company in the Revolution. One of his older sons, as has been already mentioned, was said to have cleared the site of a great town of central New York and with the pioneer urge still strong upon him to have marked the spot where a Wisconsin city now flourishes. Another kinsman lost his life in the wilderness and there was a grim report that he had fallen prey to wolves. Within my own re-

membrance the brother of our next neighbour came home
to tell of his early adventures in sending ox-teams across
the Plains from Missouri to Colorado and the dangers
from hunger, thirst, storm, and hostile Indians the task
involved. In the zeal of my youth I took him fishing; it
was a fresh southwest afternoon; he was very sick, but
took his shaking-up like a man, resolutely declaring that
he was the better for it; and the outcome of the business
was that I spent a winter on the remotest frontier of Texas,
tasting a life that warmed my heart and gave me an authentic glimpse into the country's history just as that
chapter of it was closing.

But perhaps I can best illustrate this outlook of a New
England village on the landward side by asking the reader
to walk a mile or two along the road on which my home
stood and every turn of which I knew. Beginning at the
western border and coming eastward we should soon find
the home of a man who had gone to the far Northwest
when that journey was an adventure. I well remember
hearing him tell my Father of what he saw and heard in
the territory of Washington and the especial impression
made by the size and the abundance of shell-fish on that
coast. A little further along lived a highly individual
sailor. He loved a gun as well as I and we used to meet
now and then in the salt meadows. We called him 'Captain' though I doubt if he ever rose above the rank of chief
mate. Unquestionably he had been far afield, for he had
brought home a wife from a foreign shore, he could tell of
adventures in distant seas, and his mind was so stored
with the results of a somewhat promiscuous reading —
he came of an intelligent and educated family — that I
have heard him break out with considerable declamatory
effect into a recitation of one of the great passages of the

Book of Job. I am sorry that the exact time and place
have escaped me, but the reader can imagine me in hip-
boots and old shooting coat with fowling piece upon my
shoulder standing entranced upon the bank of a tide-
creek while up from a punt in the stream below rolled the
sonorous quarter-deck voice inquiring,

> Where wast thou when I laid the foundations of the
> earth? Declare, if thou hast understanding.

There was no doubt that his appreciation of the majestic
language was real.

The next house at which we stop was a pleasant home of
seemingly well-to-do people. It became the scene of stark
tragedy which I mention from a sense of duty to my
story. Some things that have gone before might seem to
imply that I was idealising village life, and looking back
upon it through a golden haze like that which sometimes
transfigures Indian Summer landscapes. That is not the
plan of this book and the story of this particular household will bear my statement out; though I feel free to tell
it only because none of the immediate family is left to feel
hurt by the telling; and moreover it illustrates excellently
my statement that village life was always looking and often looking far beyond village bounds. The patriarch of
this home as I knew it was a strong and vigorous old man,
farmer, school-teacher, and land-surveyor — a man of
consideration in Town and Church, who, in the days of the
famous Beecher-Tilton trial in Brooklyn, had been sent
as a delegate to the Ecclesiastical Council which heard
testimony and I still think did substantial justice in the
case. One of his daughters had married a member of an
old family in a neighbouring town and had died leaving
one girl. Her youngest sister took the mother's place in

caring for the child and finally took it yet more completely by marrying the father. She was a woman plain of feature but so vital, so kind and intelligent, so humorous, and of such abounding energy, especially in all good and neighbourly offices as to be widely and deservedly beloved. To her were born four children, three sons and a daughter. All were given a good education by which they profited; and at least four of the five children developed so much taste and competence in music as to make of it either a vocation or avocation. The step-daughter became a leading teacher and the church organist. When she married a gentleman whom she met while he was visiting the town during his course at Yale and moved to another state, her eldest half-brother took her place; but only for a time as he soon passed on to become a well-known organist, choir director, and teacher of the organ in one of the more important New England cities. There he made loyal friends and seemed to prosper. The next son, feeling the urge of the West, went to Montana and became a teacher there. The younger daughter took up the task of local music-teaching and won the hearts of all she knew by her exceptional grace and charm; while the youngest son, though his vocation was that of a clerk in railway or express employ, widened his acquaintance and extended his cultural opportunity as a choir singer and soloist in a neighbouring city.

Thus the view of the family seemed wide and its prospects fair. But with the death of the grandparents it seemed as though a subsurface shrinkage had begun in its resources. The farm was neither large nor especially fruitful and the time had come when farming of the older fashion was ceasing to pay. If it were kept up at all it must be in connection with new phases of the industry, since hay, grain, and cattle were scarcely profitable. The father of the family was a town officer and a small income was probably derived from this source; but it would have been quite inadequate had not the children looked toward self-support, with something over for help to the home. Then one after another felt the hand of misfortune. The eldest daughter died in her distant home leaving two motherless boys. The second son was reported to be ill in the Far West, and when he was brought home it appeared that the illness was a 'stroke' — rare in so young and vigorous a man — which permanently and seriously crippled him. The younger daughter in what seemed to be the prime of her young womanhood went out one evening for a drive with a friend and was brought back unconscious from an apoplectic seizure of which she died within a few hours. It was scarcely to be wondered at that such a succession of sorrows should have proved too much for the mother's exceptional vigour and courage; and not very long after her daughter's death a paralytic stroke condemned her to her chair, her crutch, and her crippled knitting for the next score of years. Her remaining children were loyal and affectionate. The partially disabled son kept the place going after his father's death with admirable patience and industry; the others helped with its support.

But the story is not yet told. Suddenly and with no apparent warning almost total deafness fell upon the eldest son whose livelihood and ability to help his stricken home depended on his music. There was hope for some time that the disability might be relieved; but it proved vain, and by degrees he was forced to the conclusion that he must face a future from which his chief material resource had been cut out. A gleam of light irradiates my

story as it records the really noble loyalty of the friends
this man had made in the city where most of his professional life had been happily spent. Some sort of secretarial
work adapted to his limitations was provided, though one
suspects that much if not most of it, especially toward the
end, was 'made.' His youngest brother pursued his useful
way for some years longer, but he too fell a prey to partial
invalidism before his death. The sole survivor was the disabled second son; and neighbours sadly watched his farm
diminish and his resources dwindle. There was no way to
help it, for as his years increased, although his industry
was maintained, his judgement became clouded and his
will more stubborn. Visions of wealth in abandoned
Spanish mines floated before his eyes and tended to put
him out of conceit with friends who warned him against
delusion; until finally he gathered his few remaining possessions and departed to be no more seen and scarcely
heard of until word came of his death in a distant state.

It is a story in which blow after blow of fate falls with
the inevitability of Greek tragedy; nor was it altogether
lacking in something of the invincibility of soul that makes
true tragedy great. That 'realism' which current novelists
have reduced to a mere cant term leads me to set it down
here because of its truth, because of its suggestion of the
outlook that many a family had, and because of the reac-
tion of village life toward its incidents. There is no doubt
that these furnished gossip with interesting themes. Mr.
Arnold Bennett in one of the Five Town novels rolls its
talk about disease and progressive disability like a sweet
morsel under his 'realistic' tongue. No doubt it existed
there; as doubtless it existed here. But it was not the material fact; it was not the characteristic or the illuminating
thing. The thing to be recorded is that never during its

long experience of calamity was this family forgotten or
neglected. I do not claim that the sympathy or the material help was always adequate or perfectly adapted to
the need; it was sometimes difficult to know what to do;
yet something was always being done by relatives, neighbours, and the Church. The least adequate and satisfying
assistance was perhaps rendered to the last survivor, but
this was mainly because gradual failure sapped almost all
his powers except a stubborn will.

Our walk along this pleasant country post road, now,
alas, cemented and roaring with through-traffic, has taken
us about a mile. We shall pursue it but a quarter-mile
further. The house next to that of which I have been
speaking sent out its youngest son, first to teach and then
to enter the railway mail service. After hundreds of thousands of miles of travel he stopped long enough to oversee
for several years the transfer of mails at what was then a
railway junction of some importance; and later he became
the town's very efficient Town Clerk and Judge of Probate.
Across the street lived a retired clergyman of long and
varied experience, the friend of Horace Bushnell, for many
years one of the Fellows of Yale, and with his wife among
the chief authorities upon local history. Next again came
a large family some of whose annals have been reflected
in these pages and with whom it would be unfitting to
linger very long. Yet since we are dealing with the supposed ingrowing interests of village life it ought to be said
that when the children of this house had married and settled themselves in their various homes they represented in
themselves or their husbands the Church, Medicine, College or University Teaching, Banking, Engineering, Trade
and for many years the oversight of the family farm. This
is set down not to imply that the attainments of the fam-

ily were ever professionally eminent but to emphasise the fact that it was large enough and sufficiently varied in its interests and callings to produce a constant inflow of interesting news to such of its members as remained at home. Though the parents lived to a great age their outlook almost of necessity broadened with the years; and in this respect the family was typical of great numbers of village folk. Its mother used to remember with a sort of amused pleasure how in one year her eldest son bent upon travel and her second son on his way to become supervisor of a Philippine province touched the shores of Asia almost simultaneously, one on the west and his brother on the east; though no delusions of grandeur clouded her thought about it. She was the most sensible of women, conscious of her own limitations and of her family's, but none the less fond of remembering that two of her sons, one son-in-law and one grandson held degrees from Yale and that another son-in-law owed his bachelor's degree to Amherst and his doctorate to Johns Hopkins. It was nothing to boast about but it indicated that in the stress of home and farm work cultural interests had not altogether gone by the board. Indeed, this outlook upon the world had humorous illustration in the generation before her own; for the Grandmother of the family used to associate the birthdays of her eldest daughter and her eldest daughter-in-law with that of Queen Victoria since they fell in successive months of the same year. 'Yes,' she would say, 'Harriet was born in April, Queen Victoria in May, and Roxana in June.' It pleased her to think that 1819 had proved to be such a Year of Grace; and besides, this sequence of events provided a most convenient peg on which to hang her history.

Two doors beyond this home that has proved so diffi-

cult to pass lived an intelligent family the head of which
had belonged to the class of farmer-fishermen to whom affectionate tribute has been paid in an earlier chapter.
He had been proprietor as well as worker in that employ;
had gained an excellent education; collected a considerable
library; read it and lent the books to others; kept his cows,
his garden, and his small expanse of ploughland; inherited
a little invested property, and lived a quiet as well as
rather philosophical life with eyes and mind that were always upon the happenings of the world as well as upon
the doings of the village. I remember that one of the two
things which set him a little apart from most of his
neighbours was his learning to ride a bicycle and his habitual use of it at an age when most men would have thought
it beyond them; the other was that upon the verge of old
age he should have packed his bags and set out upon a
journey to the Mediterranean with Palestine as his especial object. It was a fine thing to do and I venture to say
that among those of his ship's company few brought to the
journey a more thoughtful mind or one better furnished
with general knowledge. By odd coincidence next to him
lived a retired school-teacher from the public schools of
New York who had come back to her childhood home, and
among whose possessions there was a little 'store.' This
had been used at one time as the branch of a somewhat
larger 'general store' in another part of town and had been
kept by a young man who grew into one of the village's
most useful citizens. Years later, after having succeeded
to the larger 'store' and retired from it with a competence,
he did very much what his late next neighbour had done —
made a Mediterranean voyage, taking with him one of
the town's perennial bachelors who had no hampering
home-ties; and again I suspect that these men who had so

long read, observed, and discussed the matters of the world amid the retirement of their village life proved as intelligent travellers as could well be found.

One more family awaits our notice. Its home was next door to the little 'store' just mentioned in an old house which had been enlarged and amply furnished. Its head was a village boy who had gone to New York, prospered there as the head of a department in one of the great 'emporia' of that early period, and come back to spend his later years amid accustomed surroundings. He farmed a good many acres and had other interests of an allied nature, in the aggregate probably not very profitable, but with means that could support them profitable or not. The family had marked mechanical talent manifest in three generations of it. Two sons and two grandsons of this branch of it went to Yale. One son died young. The other became a naval constructor long connected with the ship-building interests of Newport News.

Our walk has taken us about a mile and a quarter across an outlying school district in a town of some 1200 people at the time of which I speak. It has followed the Post Road but does not include the portion which forms the main street of the village. I have chosen it partly because of especial acquaintance with the neighbourhood and partly because it seemed to represent pretty fairly the characteristics of many a New England village of its time in its industry, its culture, and its outlook toward the world. It must be understood that this was distinctly a rural community not yet either suburbanised or become a centre of mechanical industry. Agriculture in some form was its main interest with such side issues as river, sea, and railway offered. Life had its limitations as it appears to have everywhere, most noticeably sometimes in those

regions whose people pride themselves upon a sophisti-
cated breadth scarce stopping to observe that it is in danger of becoming their only dimension. In the case of individuals it was sometimes narrow and sometimes shallow;
yet on the whole I seem to recall little resemblance to that
'Main Street' upon which Mr. Sinclair Lewis has poured
the vials of his eloquent scorn and out of which he has
coined so many convenient dollars. Its morals were not
impeccable and its taste for strong drink was quite too
urgent. Yet had Mr. Dreiser, his mouth watering for illustrations of his favourite themes, come to this town and
noted its chief characteristics I do not think he would have
found sexual irregularity or drunkenness among them,
though both were present and there were times when the
latter assumed serious proportions. The homes into which
we have looked may be regarded as showing a fair cross-
section of a town which had a distinct culture of its own,
which had a fairly intelligent historical and political outlook, which was very far indeed from being out of touch
with the world or indifferent to its affairs, and which
seems in retrospect to have been a decent place in which to
have been born and reared.

XIII

Terminus ad Quem

THE influence of the environment of youth upon maturity and age is a time-worn theme. Yet it never quite wears out and is always challenging each new generation to write its equation. This still escapes us and will do so until we define that essentially indefinable thing known as personality; which is to postpone it to the Greek Kalends. It remains none the less a profitable as well as haunting subject of man's meditation. Schelling somewhere remarks that 'The spirit has its Iliad, its tale of struggle with brutal and natural forces, and then its Odyssey, when out of its painful wanderings it returns to the Infinite.' W. J. Stillman, painter, journalist, and war correspondent, whose reminiscences indicate the exceptional width of his experience, is more concrete. He was brought up in the rather limited circle of a small Baptist sect and by a mother whose devotion to its doctrines was as strong as her life and love of her son were sincere. As the boy grew to manhood and as the man went far afield, he naturally departed somewhat widely from the views of his home. Yet he has left on record his opinion that most thoughtful men, given time enough, are likely to come back to the essential beliefs that lay at the heart of their boyhood training where this training was honest and affectionate. This is probably a too general statement; but it undoubtedly represents a not uncommon experience.

Edward FitzGerald illustrates yet another side of this experience, and one more closely akin to the theme of these chapters. Those who love his life and letters — may their tribe increase! — often lament the fact that he should so generally be known only by his translation (or paraphrase) of Omar. I read an essay upon him the other day quite in the modern manner, from which one might have gathered that the 'Rubáiyát' was a sort of testament of his opinions and a sufficient key to his character. Far more significant to me is the picture of him wandering, sometimes by day and sometimes by night, about the scenes of his birth and boyhood remembrance, or listening with a fascinated attention to the preaching of the eccentric and powerful Matthews, or at sea in their lugger with his beloved 'Posh,' or writing letters that must have pulled at the heartstrings of his correspondents as they pull at ours. What his friend Tennyson called the 'Passion of the Past' was strong upon him and it is a distinct element of his wistful power. If any reader doubt it let him read 'Bredfield Hall.' This old Suffolk mansion where he was born, where so many of the long, long thoughts of youth came and went, where his brothers and sisters were about him, where his one real love (that for the grand-daughter of the poet Crabbe) possessed him and was disappointed, made an impress on him that was never lost. He pictures the life there and those who lived it,

> Till the bell that not in vain
>   Had summoned them to weekly prayer
> Called them one by one again
>   To the church and left them there.

This may seem like a sentimental introduction to my
closing chapter. Yet it is not set down for reasons of mere
sentiment, but to illustrate rather the 'pull' which old
towns like those of which I have been speaking continue
to exercise not only upon their children but upon others
who may be separated from them by time, space, and in-
tervening generations. Much of this escapes the public's
eye. Yet it exists so really that once while resident and
officially occupied in one of these towns, I was so often applied to for answers to questions of history or genealogy
as to be compelled to arrange with a competent person to
receive and answer the inquiries as a matter of business.
One never knew why or whence such letters would come.
On one day a genealogist or antiquarian would ask for
help in tracing a man who seemed to bear the astonishing
given name of 'Nun.' To be sure it might be 'Nan'; and if
so could it have resulted as a nickname from the family
connection with Nantucket? This sort of problem demanded research with a puzzle over the uncertain script
of forgotten town clerks or old-time ministers and finally
yielded the decision that pious parents inclined to mono-
syllables had really named their son after the father of
Joshua. A town in the Middle West might yield a plea
for an ancestor who bore arms in the Indian Wars; or zeal
to be enrolled in the Daughters of the American Revolution was burning so like a fire in some feminine bones that
it could not be quenched except by the discovery of one
missing link. The clues to the link were often tenuous in
fact and likely to be confused in statement, but there was
generally a childlike confidence that a patient and good-
natured village dweller could lay his hand at once upon
Great-Great-Grandfather Abner and his record. Again,
a letter on large business paper would ask, usually suc-

cinctly and with definite clues, as to some family connection with the East. It indicated that a 'successful' man was growing old enough to look before and after even in the press of business, and that his gaze turned inevitably to the New England sources whence his family had sprung.

Moreover, as one went abroad in the land it was only to discover how many families harked back to a New England town not merely in memory but in the ordering of their life. I visited a famous preparatory school some years ago to take part in a public service and was happily entertained in the home of one of its officers and teachers who had recently brought his young wife and children from the Middle West. They were people of cultivation, refinement, and charm. But the thing that most impressed me as I stayed with them and that I have longest remembered was my feeling that I had been carried back over a generation into an atmosphere that to my lasting advantage I had breathed in youth. Here were a simplicity of manner, an unaffected piety, an honest seriousness lightened by unforced gaiety that were as refreshing as waters in the desert. The family life seemed too wholesome for the display of contempt, yet if it had appeared it would have been directed, I think, toward the cheapness and pretence of so-called 'sophistication.' And the deeply significant thing about it all was that this renewal of life came back to its old home from one of the great states of the Mississippi valley. No one can travel widely either in the older or the newer West without finding here and there little enclaves of what seem to him like rebirths of the best life his youth knew at home; and often his heart is warmed by the further discovery that the relation to the old home is recognised and happily rejoiced in. In saying this I shall of course be accused of rather smugly assuming the superiority of New England life over that of other provincial forms. That is not meant to be the attitude of these chapters. No one is quicker than the instructed New Englander to admit the charm and value of so much that distinguishes Southern life; of the contributions that the West has made, some of them distinctive and unique, others by way of modification to Eastern grafts upon its highly vigorous stock. In singing of the sound wholesomeness of apples no wise man ever means to derogate from the lusciousness of pears or the fragrance of peaches.

Nor do I mean to imply that the old strength and simplicity of typical New England village life is gone. It has been hard pressed by the incoming of foreign elements in great force and numbers; especially where communities have been highly industrialised. On the other hand it has often been the fate of the distinctly rural and agricultural communities to become suburbanised by the influx of 'summer people' as temporary or permanent residents. What they bring in the way of increased means of livelihood and often of a high understanding and true appreciation of the best in country life must not be forgotten. Yet things are never again quite the same. Perhaps they ought not to be, since, as some sage remarked the other day, a rut does not differ much from a grave except in the matter of depth. Behind and through all this change, however, much of the old New England life manages somehow to persist.

Boston, which is so often quoted as an example of a highly distinctive community that has 'gone foreign' with the influx and dominance of the Irish, is really a case in point. One would not choose to speak of the

Irish as 'foreign' did they not compel it by their clan-
nishness in politics and their tendency to dominate town
and city governments with very little regard to the
claims of civic honour. I have already spoken of the high
sense of honour with which even the very poor Irish
strove to pay their debts in the old days; and succeeded
in a degree that set them in marked contrast to many native families. I should expect that their children and
grandchildren in private matters were as worthy of their
forebears as those of native descent. But in the management of municipal affairs they have seriously smirched
their own name and the name of their race. 'Tammany'
by its conduct when the Irish influence was in the as-
cendant has become a byword and a hissing. The eager
and unremitting racial urge for office whenever an Irish
politician attains high position in either state or municipal
affairs in New England is a notorious fact and its almost
equally notorious success is a misfortune to Irish folk because it perpetuates the sense of 'foreignness' as well as
lowers the level of political life. I have myself been in-
strumental in placing Irishmen of character and influence
in positions of some importance because I thought those
of their blood and faith entitled to representation. I
should hope to do the same again should opportunity offer. But there is a distinction between a refreshing and
strengthening inflow of vigorous life and the devastation
of a racial tidal wave. From this last not a few of our
cities and some even of our villages have suffered.

It is, however, at this point that the phenomenon to
which I have just referred thrusts itself upon our notice.
The old saw that Boston is a state of mind is so time-worn
that it requires courage to repeat it; yet it contains a
truth which is rather vividly illustrated in the light of

what has just been said. Despite the lamentable influence of the Irish politician upon city government and general civic life there is something at the heart of the old town which still has its way. It not only persists but makes converts of those who rise to conquer it. Boston has, I think, put its impress upon many of the Irish as the old-time Irish themselves absorbed and made conquest of their Norman conquerors; until the Fitzgeralds outdistanced their neighbours in loyalty to the traditions and ambitions of the country. Boston has not turned the Catholic into a Protestant and is not likely to do so. The Irish have not adopted the Puritan *mores* nor are they likely to do so; though these to some extent have doubtless influenced them. Boston has done something more subtle. It has taught many of that highly imaginative race its accent. By this I do not mean of course a mere form or trick of pronunciation, though pronunciation often betrays one's birthplace and one's sympathies. I mean rather inoculation by the genius of the place. That, through the influence of historical association, schools, traditions, is by degrees having its way; and I look forward to the time when long after the Irish politician as a racial phenomenon has died and gone to his own place men and women of Irish ancestry and Irish genius shall appear to maintain the unique quality of the ancient and beloved town.

In many ways and in notable numbers children or grandchildren come back to the towns that gave them or their fathers birth. One Sunday afternoon some years ago I met upon a village street a man who had spent a long life in his birthplace. He was an excellent exemplar of a certain type of village resident. Lamed by an accident in youth, he had been forced to seek occupation at home.

But honest, intelligent, shrewd, and competent, he had found it and had served the community for many years as post-master. Old-fashioned in aspect and in speech he was none the less a fit brother to the Professor of Greek who in Yale and Trinity had established a wide reputation as a successful teacher. He too might have done the same had his path led to the university. This afternoon he was in a mood of reminiscence. We stopped and spoke. Then, after the greetings of the day, he said in his slow Yankee fashion, 'You know I have been down to the Cemetery; and they're a very quiet people there.' He spoke like one who must soon join their quietness, as indeed he did, and who looked forward to the event not only without dread but even with a sort of interest, as though being gathered to one's fathers were a lot which he would not have foregone had it been in his power. As one grows older the old-fashioned 'burying-ground' grows in its appeal. It is not only the resting-place of 'very quiet people' as my friend found it. It is the repository of village history; it is the revealer of family connections; it links the generations; its modest cenotaphs tell of men who fell in battle but whose bodies were not found or who were swallowed by the sea, or, with noticeable frequency in seaboard villages, who died of yellow fever in the West Indies or our own southern ports.

It is this general return of the absent, whether in body or only in memory to join their families that distinguishes these old towns. I used sometimes to take a relative to visit an acquaintance in Florida and while the conference went on sometimes walked in the little cemetery. Good trees were about it and the clean Florida sand possessed it. It was not a sad place in which to be left when life's tasks were done except for one thing — which was its appalling discontinuity. There was no linking of the generations; no suggestion of family history; little intimation beyond the lonesome grave of an occasional child that a home ever existed in the neighbourhood. There seemed to be merely a few old folk and a few children with a dearth of links between. I came back to study the plain brown-stone tablets marking the grave in my own family plot of an ancestor born in Oliver Cromwell's time and the place seemed homelike. The very paragraphs which I am writing must close a morning's work in time for attendance upon the funeral of an old lady whose body comes back to the town where she was born over eighty years ago. Her place is waiting in the family plot. Her father, the gratefully remembered physician of the community, lies there, her mother beside him. One son who died on the southwestern frontier came back long ago. So did the ashes of her brother, journalist and librarian in a great city in western New York. So, some day, may a remaining son who will be absent this afternoon in command of a ship which is surveying the depths and tracing the currents of the Atlantic.

A half-dozen miles away in a far more ancient cemetery a brown-stone canopy covers the grave of an English lady who came in the dawn of the village life from her old-country home. Her husband represented the proprietors of what was meant to be a considerable settlement and to reflect the distinctions of rank which marked the English society of Charles I's day. The little settlement on Saybrook Point is said to have been the first town plot in New England laid out by regular plan instead of being the victim of a Topsy-like growth; and this is probable enough, since the builder and commander of the fort was an engineer experienced in the Low Country wars. Here Lady

Fenwick lived out the brief remainder of her life, happily
enough we hope, with her husband, her little daughter,
her garden, and her exercise with horse, dog, and fowling
piece; here probably in 1645 soon after the arrival of a
second daughter born on the 4th November of that year,
she died. Her burial-place was within the fortified area of
the settlement and when 225 years later there was danger
that railway work might desecrate the grave, steps were
taken by the community to have it moved to a more
sheltered and fitting place. My Grandfather who had a
strong antiquarian bent and was a prime mover in the en-
terprise was entrusted with the attempt to recover the
remains. My Father seconded him, and with one or two
workmen, men of English birth it may be fittingly noted,
on the morning of the 18th November, 1870, opened the
grave. There were skeptics who rather scornfully insisted
that nothing would be found. But the men had not been
at work very long when one of them discovered signs in-
dicating that the remains were indeed there. My Father
then went into the grave and with the utmost care ex-
plored its depths. The coffin had completely disintegrated
except for a fragment or two adhering to the screws with
which it had been secured. But his diligent search revealed almost every bone of the skeleton and most
remarkable of all, a mass of auburn hair which seemed intact though he was compelled to exercise great care in
lifting it to prevent its coils from breaking. The skeleton
was rearticulated or at least arranged by Doctor John
Granniss, a public service very largely attended was con-
ducted by the minister of the town's historic Church, and
the mortal remains of the good lady were reverently re-
buried in its oldest cemetery within sight of her former
home. Long afterward, for no especial news of the event

had been sent to the Fenwick family in England, a most gracious letter of appreciation was received by my Father from a prominent member of it, a retired Indian officer. It is perhaps worth noting as indicative of the continuity of family history in Old and New England alike that the letter was written by Colonel George Fenwick and that its recipient was Robert Chapman; and that these were exactly the names of the representatives of the two families who were resident in the infant settlement when Lady Fenwick died almost three hundred years ago; though the first Colonel Fenwick did not receive his military title until his return to England after his wife's death. Stoke Poges is not the only Country Churchyard which moves the visitor to elegy though none other has had the benefit of Thomas Gray's melodious and wistful verses. This ancient burying ground beside the Connecticut must not detain us longer though it still sends out its call far and wide for the town's children to return.

There are other returns that the children of these towns make besides those in search of ancestry, or 'quaintness,' or the supposed romance of early colonial life, or the 'local colour' which sometimes is made up for strangers very much as antique furniture is made, or to find a resting-place for the body when the life has fled. One of the most haunting of these is the fashion in which early associations will come back as a sort of criterion or basis for judgement when one is in circumstances differing almost *in toto* from those that surrounded youth. In illustrating this I shall be forced to draw upon personal experience rather farther than could be wished; and to hark back to a reference already made to the Town Meeting and the English Parliament. On my first voyage to England I was privileged to spend parts of three days in the Speaker's

Gallery of the House of Commons [1] and one afternoon 'under the Gallery,' practically though not technically upon the floor of the House; and seven years later the privilege was almost exactly duplicated. These were exceedingly rewarding days. On one of them I heard Mr. Chamberlain read to a crowded and very solemn house the telegram announcing that the Jameson Raiders had been condemned to death in South Africa — a sentence which was not, of course, carried out. On another, seven years later, I listened to debate upon the Transvaal Loan looking toward an organisation of the country after the Boer War; and it was like hearing at first hand the beginning and end of a chapter of history. Once a question of procedure called up the notable men on both sides of the House for brief speeches and again debate on an Irish Land Bill gave the eloquence of the Irish party full sway; and very good it was. But the men were always more interesting than the speaking; and my reason for citing this experience is that the old Town Meeting memories kept thronging in to establish their parallels between the little and the great. Some readers will smile; but in point of fact the New England Town Meeting is as really a Mother of Parliaments as her great Elder Sister at Westminster. The experience in self-government and the willingness to hear many men of many minds thresh out things of public moment in free conference was, I believe, of inestimable worth to New England and to the Nation.

As I have intimated earlier most of the types in the great assembly were present first or last in the lesser one.

---

[1] I am aware that 'Speaker's Gallery' is not quite technically correct. But it indicates the special privilege that I enjoyed, and it is better to make a slight technical error than to say 'the Distinguished Strangers' Gallery' and be forced to face the question, 'What business had you there?'

I once heard Mr. Labouchere bait the Tories until some of the hapless (and helpless) gentlemen opposite were ready to foam at the mouth. 'Did you ever know his counterpart in town affairs?' I may be incredulously asked. Yes, just once, in the person of a clever, temperamental, and well-educated man whose gift for banter sometimes too recklessly exercised made him in some ways the unquestionable analogue of the militant editor of 'Truth.' I have on one or two occasions caused the adjournment of meetings in order that the effervescence of his acid playing upon alkaline opponents might subside. Of a very different sort was the impression made by my hearing of Sir Edward Grey. He was then far less of a world figure than he became ten years later in the stress of 1913–14, and I venture to quote a hurried sentence or two from my journal for the sake of a contemporaneous impression.

> Then came Sir Edward Grey whom I was very glad to hear and who made a most favourable impression. Rather awkward in manner, or perhaps I should say in gesture, he yet seemed to be perfectly at ease in every other respect. The grace and good temper of his speech were entirely germane to the man, one would have said. And there was matter in the speech too.... Sir Edward Grey spoke of the Bill (It was the Irish Land Act of 1903 and the Debate was on its Second Reading) as bringing at least the promise *of composure and reason* to the consideration of the Land Problem. I thought composure and reason to be among the leading characteristics of his address.

Composure and reason admirably describe the qualities that characterised the best speaking and that finally had their way in the best of our town meetings and that helped the later judgements of some of us as we went abroad into the world.

We had opportunity also in town affairs to judge men by something other than personal appearance and manner, though the lessons learned there were not always easy to apply; and here I have occasion to burn a penitential faggot. It was in Rome in 1913. A great and admirably appointed dinner was in process in honour of the arrival of a considerable group of Americans some on strictly official and some on semi-official business. Among these was a Congressman from an inland state whose disregard of the ordinary amenities of life in respect of dress and manner was appalling. I do not think that he meant intentionally to flout the decencies of society, but when a man on official business and therefore in a representative capacity appears in the lobby of a continental hotel on a hot evening in his shirt-sleeves and without his collar to respond to some call upon him, he needs to be reminded that this sort of thing 'isn't done' by instructed people. He could do it, and my feeling that he was likely to be called upon at this public dinner to return thanks for the courtesy extended to us may be imagined. The Mayor of Rome, Sig. Nathan, had just spoken not only in English but in admirably phrased and cadenced English, from which he turned to an Italian peroration quite as accomplished; nor was he beyond showing a little self-satisfaction in his ability to make so graceful a transition. Then my Congressman rose while a rather creepy sensation ran up and down my spine. He not only rose but began a speech of thanks so appropriately phrased, so free from fustian, so brief and fitted to the occasion that it was hard to say whether the sigh of grateful relief which went up from some of his countrymen was a tribute to his real ability or a token of the impression which he too often made. He was a most industrious and conscientious worker and I ought to have remembered some of the lessons of my boyhood better.

Yet my concern for him was as nothing to my concern for myself when called upon to perform a like task in Vienna some weeks later. The atmosphere was electric everywhere in Europe in the year before the War. The traveller in Italy and Hungary felt it especially if he were in touch with embassy, legation, or consulate; but in Austria and Germany the air was actually prickly and one knew that the least reference to international affairs was so dangerous that the only rule was to avoid it altogether. No one knew of course what the next year was to bring; but every instructed person while in Central Europe must have felt the need of weighing words and heeding steps. The dinner was in the really magnificent hall of the Rathaus. It was in substance, service, and attendance what one naturally expected of Vienna in the days before the deluge of war. So was the music; and so were the staging and singing of 'Aïda,' to which we were bidden a little later. The intelligent and informed Hungarian gentleman who was my neighbour may well have thought me a little preoccupied at times, for despite a search with prayer and fasting for a decent opening none had yet appeared. It was the music that brought salvation — that and an upbringing in a New England village. The theme of the Austrian National Anthem naturally occurred and recurred in it; and when, in thanking our hosts for all that had been done and was being done for us, I told them that Haydn's music was written in all our hymnbooks, sung in all our churches, and taught to multitudes of our children under the name of 'Austria'; and that from earliest childhood some of us had known and loved the legends of the Danube, the thing somehow got itself done. This was the

sort of international reference to which embassies and lega-
tions could take no exception; and when later in the evening Baron Von Ehrenfels tried to be kind about it, I
knew that my early acquaintance with a New England
hymnbook and the very poor library of a district school
had not been altogether in vain. I attended a district
school for only a term or two while my private school was
in abeyance; its library was both scanty and ill chosen;
but it did have a copy of de la Motte Fouqué's 'Undine';
I think his 'Sintram' was bound with it; and I long cherished a boyish wonder as to who Baron de la Motte Fouqué might be.

It was a fateful summer. We did not know it, but in
point of fact we had come to the End of the World and
were looking over its edge. We were presented to the
King and Queen of Italy with no Mussolini in the background; to President and Madame Poincaré in the great
rooms of the Elysée with no suspicion of the Red Sea of
Verdun, so soon to be crossed; and we went to a tea — of
all places in the world — in the Gilded Chamber of the
Bank of France where the grave financiers, seen again in
memory, still raise a smile as I think of the contrast they
presented to the accepted notion that so many English
and Americans have of typical Frenchmen. I even noted
in my journal the resemblance of the Governor to a man
whom I knew well and held in high regard in the Old Saybrook days — as typical and as modest a New Englander
as one could wish to meet. It is only as I think of the little
room in the Uffizi in Florence where the mature work of
Perugino stands side by side with the early painting of his
greater pupil Raphael, each illuminating the other; or of
St. Peter's with folk of every race passing to and fro
across its pavements; or of the mighty spire of Ulm parish

church as one looks out on the way from Munich to Stutt-
gart; or, in a very different setting, of a Hungarian village
with its men and women toiling in the fields, its little com-
munal enterprises, its co-operative endeavours after mutual help in procuring supplies, selling produce, and insur-
ing poor possessions against the change and chance of
tomorrow — it is only then in the presence of religion,
art, and the struggle of plain folk toward mutual understanding and support, that I seem to be in the presence of
something that will either abide as it is or exert deep and
permanent influence upon tomorrow. And in it all there
was natural and happy reference to the experience and the
principles furnished by a boyhood in a New England
village.

It may not be unfitting to ask in closing whether in
such a journey as this which brought us into unusual contact with the life and ways of plain people we gained any
glimpse of hope for the future on the other side of the
abyss that yawned so near our feet though obscured from
our eyes. We have since heard much of the certain dis-
solution of Civilisation should another war occur; and I
confess to some surprise at the scepticism about the reality
or possibility of progress which has been so general since
the War. I do not believe that Civilisation will consent to
be so easily dismissed; nor that Progress is a mere will-o'-
the-wisp meant to tickle our vanity and lead our deluded
feet into a Slough of Despond. In thinking of Progress we
have been guilty of two mistakes. We have inclined to
define it far too much in terms of mere physical con-
venience, comfort, and well-being. We have thought of
our ingenuities as its prime ministers. Because we have in
America brought those indispensable nuisances, the automobile, the telephone, and the radio within the reach of

such multitudes we flatter ourselves that we by so much
lead the world; or at any rate that we have got on very
creditably. Measured by the automobile and bathroom
standard we have. But the standard leaves so much to be
desired. The college President who asked his students the
other day as to the use of talking across the continent if
one had nothing pertinent to say, or travelling from one
place to another at high speed if one were as restless at
the end of the journey as at its start, or crossing the ocean
with ease and safety in the hope of escaping conscience,
was putting old-fashioned but exceedingly pertinent questions. The fundamental problems relating to human
happiness and to any progress worth having are still
predominantly ethical. I believe in progress in this realm.
But the man who pictures it in terms of the inclined plane
trending steadily upward or of the spiral with its frequent
and sometimes confusing change of direction but still
with steady upward trend, fails seriously in making his
figure fit the facts. I prefer to go back to old days and old
sea scenes. How many times I have seen a vessel going up-
Sound with wind and tide both in her favour and making
the bravest of progress. But how many more times have
I seen craft making the best of circumstance that was
only with her in part, a favouring tide perhaps but a wind
that compelled her to beat up against it, making progress
by means of a force that if unconstrained by human intelligence must have driven her back to defeat of present
purpose and possibly to destruction; yet with a great
favouring trend beneath her that helped her on. Again,
with the wind still against her, the flood turned to ebb.
There was little progress now; only a determined beating
up against what seemed for the time a hostile destiny,
just holding her own, perhaps even losing on this tack or

that, until, if in soundings that made it practicable, the best thing was often to anchor and simply hold on until tide or wind favoured again. Human progress is like that. Yet ships got on. The great majority of them made port. And not a few of those who seemed to fail and perish by the way might have chosen for themselves the epitaph from the old Greek anthology,

> A shipwrecked sailor buried on this coast
>   Bids you set sail.
> Full many a gallant barque when we were lost
>   Weathered the gale.

So long as a man is left to think clearly and act with courage the cause of progress is not lost and the activities that make for conquest of circumstance will be maintained. That was the doctrine that undergirded the best village life in the New England that I knew. I still think it sound.